1,000,000 Books

are available to read at

www.ForgottenBooks.com

Read online
Download PDF
Purchase in print

ISBN 978-0-243-30921-4
PIBN 10793030

This book is a reproduction of an important historical work. Forgotten Books uses state-of-the-art technology to digitally reconstruct the work, preserving the original format whilst repairing imperfections present in the aged copy. In rare cases, an imperfection in the original, such as a blemish or missing page, may be replicated in our edition. We do, however, repair the vast majority of imperfections successfully; any imperfections that remain are intentionally left to preserve the state of such historical works.

Forgotten Books is a registered trademark of FB &c Ltd.
Copyright © 2018 FB &c Ltd.
FB &c Ltd, Dalton House, 60 Windsor Avenue, London, SW19 2RR.
Company number 08720141. Registered in England and Wales.

For support please visit www.forgottenbooks.com

1 MONTH OF FREE READING

at

www.ForgottenBooks.com

By purchasing this book you are eligible for one month membership to ForgottenBooks.com, giving you unlimited access to our entire collection of over 1,000,000 titles via our web site and mobile apps.

To claim your free month visit:
www.forgottenbooks.com/free793030

* Offer is valid for 45 days from date of purchase. Terms and conditions apply.

English
Français
Deutsche
Italiano
Español
Português

www.forgottenbooks.com

Mythology Photography **Fiction** Fishing Christianity **Art** Cooking Essays Buddhism Freemasonry Medicine **Biology** Music **Ancient Egypt** Evolution Carpentry Physics Dance Geology **Mathematics** Fitness Shakespeare **Folklore** Yoga Marketing **Confidence** Immortality Biographies Poetry **Psychology** Witchcraft Electronics Chemistry History **Law** Accounting **Philosophy** Anthropology Alchemy Drama Quantum Mechanics Atheism Sexual Health **Ancient History Entrepreneurship** Languages Sport Paleontology Needlework Islam **Metaphysics** Investment Archaeology Parenting Statistics Criminology **Motivational**

ΠΡΟΓΥΜΝΑΣΜΑΤΑ.

PASSAGES IN PROSE AND VERSE

FROM ENGLISH AUTHORS

FOR

TRANSLATION INTO GREEK AND LATIN;

TOGETHER WITH

SELECTED PASSAGES FROM GREEK AND LATIN AUTHORS

FOR TRANSLATION INTO ENGLISH:

FORMING

A REGULAR COURSE OF EXERCISES IN CLASSICAL COMPOSITION.

BY THE

Rev. HENRY ALFORD, M.A.,

VICAR OF WYMESWOLD, LEICESTERSHIRE, AND
LATE FELLOW OF TRINITY COLLEGE, CAMBRIDGE.

CAMBRIDGE:
PRINTED AT THE UNIVERSITY PRESS,
FOR J. AND J. J. DEIGHTON;
AND SOLD BY
WHITTAKER & CO.; SIMPKIN, MARSHALL & CO.; AND GEORGE BELL,
LONDON.

11552
22/12/90

INTRODUCTION.

The object of this Volume is to furnish Private Tutors and Masters of the higher forms in Schools, with a regular course of composition in which to exercise their Pupils. The pieces have been selected by the Editor for his own use, and have, many of them, undergone the test of frequent translation.

It has been thought desirable to intersperse with the composition, passages from Greek and Latin authors for translation into English. These are not given at length, but merely referred to, as the books are in every one's hands; and their selection usually has reference to the pieces for composition which follow them.

The student is recommended to prepare for composing in Greek or Latin, by reading (if aloud, the better) for about half an hour from some classical author, whose subject and manner of writing may be similar to that prescribed to him. Thus he will catch the spirit and tone of thought of the best days of the language; and, if he be writing in verse, will fall into an easy and unfettered style. He should not, however, degenerate into mere imitation: it is not the object of the scholar to parody Herodotus, or Euripides, Livy, or Lucretius, but to express the subject matter set before him in elegant diction, and with manly freedom, in the languages in which these authors wrote.

The student cannot be too strongly cautioned against the use of those nuisances, English Latin, and Latin Greek dictionaries. *Neither of these should ever be used.* They cannot possibly give the word exactly corresponding to that in the text, in the meaning which it there bears. When a difficulty occurs in expressing a word in Greek or Latin, let the memory be well ransacked to solve it: if this fail, let a blank be left for the tutor to supply. If the word thought of be doubtful, let the dictionary be consulted, but let it be to find by examples, whether the *Latin or Greek word* will bear the sense which it is proposed to give to it.

Another rule, hardly ever enough observed by young composers, is, to translate the *sense* of the sentence, not *its English form*. The neglect of this, by rendering clause after clause as they occur, leads, even where ludicrous Anglicisms are avoided, to unpleasing and unclassical versions. Each sentence should be well conned over in the mind, divested of its idiomatic form, and reduced to its elements of thought: while all the time its general cast is preserved, and the Latin or Greek version, when made, is not the same thought *otherwise* expressed, but the correlative expression of it in another language and another age.

And if this is the case in prose, much more is it in poetry. The whole cast of an English stanza or couplet must sometimes be changed before it is capable of expression in Latin or Greek: and he is the true master of compositiou who can so do this as to preserve the same features and the same minor associations still.

In the case of Greek Iambics, the Indices to the Tragedians should be judiciously, and but sparingly, used. Nothing can be less desirable than the practice of making copies of Iambics which are mere centos from the Tragedians. Here, as always, composition should be consistent, manly, and independent, not of rules, but of servile imitation.

And, in general, let the student remember that composition, like every other art, consists in employing the powers of invention and expression according to certain rules: that the material in which his ideas must be expressed is, the language of certain authors during a certain period: and that the rules by which he must be guided are the proprieties of diction and sanctions of usage then prevalent among those writers.

WYMESWOLD, *Oct.* 1, 1845.

PASSAGES FOR TRANSLATION

IN PROSE AND VERSE.

Into Latin Prose.

CÆSAR, now within sight of Britain, beholds on every hill multitudes of armed men, ready to forbid his landing; and Cicero writes to his friend Atticus, that the accesses of the island were wonderously fortified with strong works or moles. Here from the fourth to the ninth hour of day he awaits at anchor the coming up of his whole fleet; meanwhile with his legates and tribunes consulting and giving order to fit all things for what might happen in such a various and floating water-fight as was to be expected. This place, which was a narrow bay, close environed with hills, appearing no way commodious, he removes to a plain and open shore eight miles distant, commonly supposed about Deal, in Kent. Which when the Britons perceived, their horse and chariots, as then they used in fight, scouring before, their main power speeding after, some thick upon the shore, others not tarrying to be assailed, ride in among the waves to encounter, and assault the Romans, even under their ships, with such a bold and free hardihood, that Cæsar himself between confessing and excusing that his soldiers were to come down from their ships, to stand in water heavy armed, and to fight at once, denies not but that the terror of such new and resolute opposition made them forget their wonted valour—to succour which he commands his galleys, a sight unusual to the

Britons, and more apt for motion, drawn from the bigger vessels, to row against the open side of the enemy, and thence with slings, engines, and darts, to beat them back. But neither yet, though amazed at the strangeness of those new sea-castles bearing up so near, and so swiftly as almost to overwhelm them; the hurtling of oars, the battering of fierce engines against their bodies, barely exposed, did the Britons give much ground, or the Romans gain; till he who bore the eagle of the tenth legion, yet in the galleys, first beseeching his gods, said thus aloud, "Leap down, soldiers, unless ye mean to betray your ensign; I for my part will perform what I owe to the commonwealth and my general." This uttered, overboard he leaps, and with his eagle fiercely advanced runs upon the enemy; the rest heartning one another not to admit the dishonour of so nigh losing their chief standard, follow him resolutely.

Translate THUCYDIDES, *Book* II. *Chap.* 4.

Into Latin Elegiacs.

Now that all hearts are glad, all faces bright,
  Our aged sovereign sits; to the ebb and flow
Of states and kingdoms, to their joy or woe,
  Insensible; he sits deprived of sight,
And lamentably wrapt in twofold night,
  Whom no weak hopes deceived; whose mind ensued,
Through perilous war, with regal fortitude,
  Peace that should claim respect from lawless might.
Dread King of kings, vouchsafe a ray divine
  To his forlorn condition! let thy grace

Upon his inner soul in mercy shine;
Permit his heart to kindle, and embrace
(Though it were only for a moment's space)
The triumphs of this hour; for they are *Thine!* +

Translate TACITUS, *Annal.* I. *Chaps.* 42, 43.

Into Greek Prose.

WORTHY deeds are not often destitute of worthy relaters: as by a certain fate, great acts and great eloquence have most commonly gone hand in hand, equalling and honouring each other in the same ages. 'Tis true, that in obscurest times, by shallow and unskilful writers, the indistinct noise of many battles, and devastations of many kingdoms overrun and lost, hath come to our ears. For what wonder, if in all ages, ambition and the love of rapine hath stirred up greedy and violent men to bold attempts in wasting and ruining wars, which to posterity have left the work of wild beasts and destroyers, rather than the deeds and monuments of men and conquerors? But he whose true and just valour uses the necessity of war and dominion not to destroy but to prevent destruction; to bring in liberty against tyrants, law and civility among barbarous nations, knowing that when he conquers all things else, he cannot conquer *Time* or *Detraction*, wisely conscious of this his want as well as of his worth not to be forgotten or concealed, honours, and hath recourse to the aid of eloquence, his friendliest and best supply; by whose immortal record his noble deeds, which else were transitory, becoming fixt and durable against the force of years and generations, he fails not to continue through all posterity, over envy, death, and time also, victorious.

Into Latin Lyrics.

To the ocean now I fly,
And those happy climes that lie
Where day never shuts his eye,
Up in the broad fields of the sky:
There I suck the liquid air
All amidst the gardens fair
Of Hesperus, and his daughters three
That sing about the golden tree:
Along the crisped shades and bowers
Revels the spruce and jocund spring,
The graces, and the rosy-bosom'd hours,
Thither all their bounties bring;
There eternal summer dwells,
And west winds, with musky wing,
About the cedran alleys fling
Nard and cassia's balmy smells.
Iris there with humid bow
Waters the odorous banks, that blow
Flowers of more mingled hue
Than her purpled scarf can show,
And drenches with Elysian dew
(List, mortals, if your ears be true)
Beds of hyacinth and roses,
Where young Adonis oft reposes,
Waxing well of his deep wounds
In slumber soft, and on the ground
Sadly sits th' Assyrian queen;
But far above in spangled sheen
Celestial Cupid, her fam'd son advanc'd,
Holds his dear Psyche sweet intranc'd
After her wand'ring labours long,

'Till free consent the gods among
Make her his eternal bride,
And from her fair unspotted side
Two blissful twins are to be born,
Youth and Joy; so Jove hath sworn.

Translate SOPHOCLES, *Œdipus Coloneus* (*ed.* Hermann), *from* v. 259. τί δῆτα .... *to* v. 292. γίγνου κακός.

Into Greek Prose.

✝ ARCHIDAMUS, king of Sparta, now about to march against us, is bound to me by the laws of hospitality. Should he, whether in remembrance of these, or in the design of rendering me suspected, abstain from inflicting on my possessions the violence he is about to inflict on the rest of Attica, let it be understood that henceforth I have no private property in this land, but, in the presence of the gods, make a free donation of it to the commonwealth. Let all withdraw their cattle, corn, and other effects, from the country, and hold Athens as one great citadel, from which the deity, who presides over her, hath forbidden us to descend. ✝

Translate HORACE, *de Arte Poetica*, vv. 366—390.

Into Latin Hexameters.

ANOTHER part in squadrons and gross bands,
On bold adventure to discover wide

That dismal world, if any clime perhaps
Might yield them easier habitation, bend
Four ways their flying march, along the banks
Of four infernal rivers, that disgorge
Into the burning lake their baleful streams:
Abhorred Styx, the flood of deadly hate;
Sad Acheron of sorrow, black and deep;
Cocytus, nam'd of lamentation loud
Heard on the rueful stream; fierce Phlegeton,
Whose waves of torrent fire inflame with rage.
Far off from these a slow and silent stream,
Lethe the river of oblivion, rolls
Her wat'ry labyrinth, whereof who drinks,
Forthwith his former state and being forgets—
Forgets both joy and grief, pleasure and pain.
Beyond this flood a frozen continent
Lies, dark and wild, beat with perpetual storms
Of whirlwind and dire hail; which on firm land
Thaws not, but gathers heap, and ruin seems
Of ancient pile; all else deep snow and ice;
A gulf profound as that Serbonian bog
Betwixt Damietta and mount Casius old,
Where armies whole have sunk; the parching air
Burns frore, and cold performs th' effect of fire—
Part, on the plain, or in the air sublime
Upon the wing, or in swift race contend,
As at the Olympian games, or Pythian fields;
Part curb their fiery steeds, or shun the goal
With rapid wheels, or fronted brigads form.
As when, to warn proud cities, war appears
Wag'd in the troubled sky, and armies rush
To battel in the clouds, before each van
Prick forth the aery knights, and couch their spears

'Till thickest legions close; with feats of arms
From either end of heav'n the welkin burns.
Others with vast Typhœan rage more fell
Rend up both rocks and hills, and ride the air
In whirlwind: hell scarce holds the wild uproar.
As when Alcides from Œchalia crown'd
With conquest, felt th' envenom'd robe, and tore
Through pain up by the roots Thessalian pines,
And Lichas from the top of Æta threw
Into th' Euboic sea.

Into Latin Prose.

WHILE these things are doing, one of the legions being sent out to forage, as was accustomed, and no suspicion of war, while some of the Britons were remaining in the country about, others also going and coming freely to the Roman quarters, they who were in station at the camp-gates sent speedy word to Cæsar, that, from that part of the country to which the legion went, a greater dust than usual was seen to rise. Cæsar, guessing the matter, commands the cohorts of guard to follow him thither, two others to succeed in their stead, the rest all to arm and follow. They had not marched long, when Cæsar discerns his legion sore over-charged: for the Britons, not doubting but that their enemies on the morrow would be in that place which only they had left unreaped of all their harvest, had placed an ambush; and while they were dispersed and busiest at their labour, set upon them, killed some, and routed the rest. The manner of their fight was from a kind of chariot, wherein riding about, and throwing darts, with the clatter of their horse, and of their wheels, they oft-times broke the rank of their enemies: then retreating among the horse and quitting their chariots, they fought on foot. The charioteers in the meanwhile, somewhat aside from the battle, set themselves in such order that their masters, at any time oppressed with odds, might retire safely thither, having performed with one person both the nimble service of a horseman and the steadfast duty of a foot-soldier. So much they could with their chariots by use and exercise, as riding on the speed down a steep hill, to stop suddenly, and with a short rein turn swiftly, now running on the beam, now on the yoke, then in the seat.

Into Greek Iambics.

BACCHUS, that first from out the purple grape
Crush'd the sweet poison of misused wine,
After the Tuscan mariners transform'd,
Coasting the Tyrrhene shore, as the winds listed,
On Circe's island fell: who knows not Circe,
The daughter of the Sun, whose charmed cup
Whoever tasted, lost his upright shape,
And downward fell into a grovelling swine?
This nymph that gazed upon his clust'ring locks,
With ivy-berries wreath'd, and his blithe youth,
Had by him, ere he parted thence, a son
Much like his father, but his mother more,
Whom therefore she brought up, and Comus nam'd:
Who ripe, and frolic of his full-grown age,
Roving the Celtic and Iberian fields,
At last betakes him to this ominous wood,
And in thick shelter of black shades imbower'd
Excels his mother at her mighty art,
Offering to every weary traveller
His orient liquor in a crystal glass,

To quench the drouth of Phœbus, which as they taste,
(For most do taste through fond intemp'rate thirst)
Soon as the potion works, their human count'nance,
Th' express resemblance of the Gods, is chang'd
Into some brutish form of wolf, or bear,
Or ounce, or tiger, hog, or bearded goat,
All other parts remaining as they were;
And they so perfect in their misery,
Not once perceive their foul disfigurement,
But boast themselves more comely than before,
And all their friends and native home forget,
To roll with pleasure in a sensual stye.

Translate TACITUS, *Annal. Book* VI. *Chaps.* 20—22.

Into Latin Prose.

✓ IF a man were called to fix the period in the history of the world, during which the condition of the human race was most happy and prosperous, he would, without hesitation, name that which elapsed from the death of Domitian to the accession of Commodus. The vast extent of the Roman Empire was governed by absolute power, under the guidance of virtue and wisdom. The armies were restrained by the firm but gentle hand of four successive emperors, whose characters and authority commanded involuntary respect. The forms of the civil administration were carefully preserved by Nerva, Trajan, Hadrian, and the Antonines, who delighted in the image of liberty, and were pleased with considering themselves as the accountable ministers of the laws. Such princes deserved the honour of restoring the republic, had the Romans of their days been capable of enjoying a rational freedom.

Translate SOPHOCLES *Ajax* (*ed.* Hermann), v. 802,
ὁ μὲν σφαγεὺς ... *to* v. 852, μυθήσομαι.

Into Latin Alcaics.

WHILE not a leaf seems faded—while the fields
With ripening harvest prodigally fair,
In brightest sunshine bask—this nipping air,
Sent from some distant clime where Winter wields
His icy scimitar, a foretaste yields
Of bitter change—and bids the flowers beware;
And whispers to the silent birds, "Prepare
Against the threatening foe your trustiest shields"
For me, who under kindlier laws belong
To Nature's tuneful quire, this rustling dry
Through leaves yet green, and yon crystalline sky,
Announce a season potent to renew,
Mid frost and snow, the instinctive joys of song,
And nobler cares than listless summer knew.

Translate HERODOTUS, *Book* I. *Chap.* 126.

Into Greek Iambics.

I HAVE kept many a man, and many a great one;
Yet I confess, I never saw before
A man of such a sufferance: he lies now
Where I'd not lay my dog (for sure 'twould kill him),
Where neither light or comfort can come near him;
Nor air nor earth that's wholesome. It grieves me

To see a mighty king, with all his glory,
Sunk o' th' sudden to the bottom of a dungeon.
Whither should we descend that are poor rascals,
If we had our deserts? 'Tis a strange wonder!
Load him with irons, oppress him with contempts,
(Which are the governor's commands) give him nothing,
Or so little, to sustain life 'tis next nothing,
They stir not him; he smiles upon his miseries,
And bears 'em with such strength, as if his nature
Had been nurs'd up, and foster'd with calamities.
He gives no ill words, curses, nor repines not,
Blames nothing, hopes in nothing, we can hear of;
And, in the midst of all these frights, fears nothing.

Into Latin Elegiacs.

SET me whereas the sun doth parch the green,
Or where his beams do not dissolve the ice;
In temperate heat, where he is felt and seen;
In presence prest of people, mad or wise;
Set me in high, or yet in low degree;
In longest night, or in the shortest day;
In clearest sky, or where clouds thickest be;
In lusty youth, or when my hairs are gray;
Set me in heaven, in earth, or else in hell;
In hill or dale, or in the foaming flood;
Thrall, or at large, alive whereso I dwell;
Sick, or in health, in evil frame or good;
Hers will I be, and only with this thought
Content myself, although my chance be nought.

Translate Livy's *Preface.*

Into Latin Prose.

Romulus was a just king, and gentle to his people: if any were guilty of crimes, he did not put them to death, but made them pay a fine of sheep or oxen. In his wars he was very successful, and enriched his people with the spoils of their enemies. At last, after he had reigned nearly forty years it chanced that one day he called his people together in the field of Mars near the Goats' Pool, when all on a sudden, there arose a dreadful storm, and all was dark as night; and the rain and thunder and lightning were so terrible, that all the people fled from the field, and ran to their several homes. At last the storm was over, and they came back to the field of Mars, but Romulus was nowhere to be found: for Mars, his father, had carried him up to heaven in his chariot. The people knew not at first what was become of him; but when it was night, as one Proculus Julius was coming from Alba to the city, Romulus appeared to him in more than mortal beauty, and grown to more than mortal stature, and said to him, "Go and tell my people that they weep not for me any more: but bid them to be brave and warlike, and so shall they make my city the greatest in the earth." Then the people knew that Romulus was become a god; so they built a temple to him, and offered sacrifice to him, and worshipped him evermore by the name of the God Quirinus.

Into Greek Prose, in the style of Herodotus.

THEY understood by the way, that their Chrolopey or bond-slaves, whom they left at home, had in their absence possessed their towns, lands, houses, wives, and all. At which newes being somewhat amazed, and yet disdaining the villany of their servants, they made the more speede home: and so not farre from Novograd met them in warlike manner marching against them. Whereupon advising what was best to be done, they agreed also to set upon them with no other shew of weapon, but with their horsewhips (which as their manner is, every man rideth withall) to put them in remembrance of their servile condition, thereby to terrifie them, and abate their courage. And so marching on, and lashing altogether with their whips in their hands, they gave the onset: which seemed so terrible in the eares of their villaines, and strooke such a sense into them of the smart of the whip, which they had felt before, that they fled altogether like sheepe before the drivers. In memory of this victory, the Novogradians ever since have stamped their coine (which they call a Dingoe Novogradskoy, currant through all Russia) with the figure of a horseman shaking a whip aloft in his hand. It may seeme, that all the women of that country have fared the worse ever since, in regard of the universal fault; for such a whip as terrefied those slaves, curiously wrought by herselfe, is the first present that the Muscovian wife, even in time of wooing, sends to him that shall be her husband, in token of subjection.

Translate HORACE, *Book* IV. *Ode* 4.

Into Latin Elegiacs.

Now while the night her sable veil hath spread,
And silently her resty coach doth roll,
Rousing with her from Tethys' azure bed
Those starry nymphs which dance about the pole:
While Cynthia, in purest cyprus cled,
The Latmian shepherd in a trance descries,
And whiles looks pale from height of all the skies,
Whiles dyes her beauties in a bashful red;
While Sleep, in triumph closed hath all eyes,
And birds and beasts a silence sweet do keep,
And Proteus' monstrous people in the deep
The winds and waves hush'd up to rest entice;
I wake, muse, weep, and who my heart hath slain
See still before me to augment my pain.

Into Greek or Latin Hexameters.

Together both, ere the high lawns appeared
Under the opening eyelids of the morn,
We drove a-field, and both together heard
What time the gray-fly winds her sultry horn
Batt'ning our flocks with the fresh dews of night,
Oft till the star that rose at evening, bright,
Toward heav'ns descent had slop'd his west'ring wheel.
Meanwhile the rural ditties were not mute,
Temper'd to the oaten flute,
Rough Satyrs daue'd, and Fauns with cloven heel
From the glad sound would not be absent long,
And old Damætas lov'd to hear our song—
But, O the heavy change, now thou art gone,

Now thou art gone, and never must return!
Thee, shepherd, thee the woods, and desert caves
With wild thyme, and the gadding vine o'ergrown,
And all their echoes mourn.
The willows, and the hazel copses green,
Shall now no more be seen,
Fanning their joyous leaves to thy soft lays.
As killing as the canker to the rose,
Or taint-worm to the weanling herds that graze,
Or frost to flow'rs, that their gay wardrobe wear,
When first the white-thorn blows;
Such, Lycidas, thy loss to shepherd's ear.
Where were ye, Nymphs, when the remorseless deep
Clos'd o'er the head of your lov'd Lycidas?
For neither were ye playing on the steep,
Where your old bards, the famous Druids, lie,
Nor on the shaggy top of Mona high,
Nor yet where Deva spreads her wizard stream:
Ay me! I fondly dream!—
Had ye been there, for what could that have done?
What could the muse herself that Orpheus bore,
The muse herself for her inchanting son,
Whom universal nature did lament,
When by the rout that made the hideous roar,
His gory visage down the stream was sent,
Down the swift Hebrus to the Lesbian shore?

Translate THUCYDIDES, *Book* II. *Chaps.* 37, 38.

Into Greek Prose.

THAT which we properly call Tyrannie, is,—A violent form of government, not respecting the good of the subject, but only the pleasure of the commander.—I purposely forbear to say, that it is the unjust rule of one over many: for very truely doth Cleon in Thucydides tell the Athenians, that their dominion over their subjects, was none other than a meere tyrannie; though it were so, that they themselves were a great citie and a popular estate. Neither is it peradventure greatly needful that I should call this forme of commanding, *violent:* since it may well and easily be conceived, that no man willingly performs obedience to one regardlesse of his life and welfare; unless himselfe be either a madman, or (which is little better) wholly possessed with some extreme passion of love. The practice of tyrannie is not alwaies of a like extremitie: for some lords are more gentle than others to their very slaves; and he that is most cruell to some, is milde enough towards others, though it be but for his owne advantage. Neverthelesse, in large dominions, wherein the rule's discretion cannot extend itselfe, unto notice of the difference which might be found between the worth of severall men, it is commonly seene that the taste of sweetnesse, drawne out of oppression, hath so good a rellish, as continually inflames the tyrant's appetite, and will not suffer it to be restrained with any limits of respect.

Into Latin Lyrics.

SHEPHERDS all, and maidens fair,
Fold your flocks up, for the air
'Gins to thicken, and the sun
Already his great course hath run.
See the dew-drops how they kiss
Ev'ry little flower that is;
Hanging on their velvet heads,
Like a rope of christal beads:
See the heavy clouds low falling,
And bright Hesperus down calling
The dead night from under ground;
At whose rising mists unsound,
Damps and vapours fly apace,
Hov'ring o'er the wanton face
Of these pastures, where they come
Striking dead both bud and bloom:
Therefore from such danger lock
Ev'ry one his loved flock;
And let your dogs lie loose without,
Lest the wolf come as a scout
From the mountain, and, 'ere day,
Bear a lamb, or kid away;
Or the crafty thievish fox
Break upon your simple flocks.
To secure yourselves from these,
Be not too secure in ease;
Let one eye his watches keep,
While the other eye doth sleep;
So you shall good shepherds prove,
And for ever hold the love

Of our great god. Sweetest slumbers,
And soft silence, fall in numbers
On your eye-lids! So, farewell!
Thus I end my evening's knell.

Translate EURIPIDES, *Medea*, 1015, δράσω τάδ'... *to*
1076, βροτοῖς.

Into Greek Iambics.

A LITTLE onward lend thy guiding hand
To these dark steps, a little further on;
For yonder bank hath choice of sun or shade:
There I am wont to sit, when any chance
Relieves me from my task of servile toil,
Daily in the common prison else enjoin'd me,
Where I, a prisoner chain'd, scarce freely draw
The air imprisoned also, close and damp,
Unwholesome draught: but here I feel amends,
The breath of heav'n fresh blowing, pure and sweet,
With day-spring born; here leave me to respire.
This day a solemn feast the people hold
To Dagon, their sea-idol, and forbid
Laborious works: unwillingly this rest
Their superstition yields me: hence with leave
Retiring from the popular noise, I seek
This unfrequented place to find some ease,
Ease to the body some, none to the mind
From restless thoughts, that, like a deadly swarm
Of hornets arm'd no sooner found alone,
But rush upon me thronging, and present
Times past, what once I was, and what am now.

Into Latin Hexameters.

AND now beneath the horizon westering slow
Had sunk the orb of day: o'er all the vale
A purple softness spread, save where the tree
Its giant shadow stretch'd, or winding stream
Mirror'd the light of Heaven, still traced distinct
When twilight dimly shrouded all beside.
A grateful coolness freshen'd the calm air,
And the hoarse grasshoppers their evening song
Sung shrill and ceaseless, as the dews of night
Descended. On their way the travellers wend,
Cheering the road with converse, till at length
They mark a cottage lamp, whose steady light
Shone through the lattice: thitherward they turn.
There came an old man forth: his thin grey locks
Waved on the night-breeze, and on his shrunk face
The characters of age were written deep.
Them, louting low with rustic courtesy,
He welcomed in; on the white ember'd hearth
Heapt up fresh fuel, then with friendly care
Spread out the homely board, and fill'd the bowl
With the red produce of the vine that arch'd
His evening seat; they of the plain repast
Partook, and quaff'd the pure and pleasant draught.

Translate HERODOTUS, *Book* VII. *Chaps.* 63, 64.

Into Latin Prose.

So long and so various was the pomp of Aurelian's triumph, that, although it opened with the dawn of day, the slow majesty of the procession ascended not the capitol before the ninth hour; and it was already dark when the emperor returned to the palace. The festival was protracted by the theatrical representations, the games of the circus, the hunting of wild beasts, combats of gladiators, and naval engagements. Liberal donatives were distributed to the army and people, and several institutions, agreeable or beneficial to the city, contributed to perpetuate the glory of Aurelian. A considerable portion of his oriental spoils was consecrated to the gods of Rome; the capitol, and every other temple, glittered with the offerings of his ostentatious piety; and the temple of the Sun alone received above fifteen thousand pounds of gold. This last was a magnificent structure, erected by the emperor on the side of the Quirinal hill, and dedicated, soon after the triumph, to that deity whom Aurelian adored as the parent of his life and fortunes. His mother had been an inferior priestess in a chapel of the Sun: a peculiar devotion to the god of light, was a sentiment which the fortunate peasant imbibed in his infancy; and every step of his elevation, every victory of his reign, fortified superstition by gratitude.

Into Latin Lyrics.

Fond words have oft been spoken to thee, Sleep!
And thou hast had thy store of tenderest names;
The very sweetest words that fancy frames,
When thankfulness of heart is strong and deep!
Dear bosom-child we call thee, that dost steep
In rich reward all suffering; balm that tames
All anguish; saint, that evil thoughts and aims
Takest away, and into souls dost creep,
Like to a breeze from heaven. Shall I alone,

I surely not a man ungently made,
Call thee worst tyrant by which flesh is crost?
Perverse, self-willed, to own and to disown,
Mere slave of them who never for thee prayed,
Still last to come where thou art wanted most!

Into Greek Iambics, or Latin Hexameters.

So spake the seraph Abdiel, faithful found
Among the faithless, faithful only he:
Among innumerable false unmov'd,
Unshaken, unseduced, unterrify'd,
His loyalty he kept, his love, his zeal;
Nor number, nor example with him wrought
To swerve from truth, or change his constant mind
Though single. From amidst them forth he pass'd
Long way through hostile scorn, which he sustain'd
Superior, nor of violence fear'd aught:
And with retorted scorn his back he turu'd
On those proud tow'rs to swift destruction doom'd.

Translate LIVY, *Book* I. *Chap.* 54.

Into Latin Elegiacs.

As when to seeke her foode abroad doth rove
The nuncius of peace, the seely dove,
Two sharpe-set hawkes doe her on each side hem,
And she knows not which way to flye from them:
Or like a shippe that tossed to and fro
With winde and tyde, the winde doth sternely blow,
And drives her to the maine, the tyde comes sore,

And hurles her backe againe towards the shore;
And since her balast and her sailes do lacke,
One brings her out, the other beates her backe;
Till one of them encreasing more his shockes,
Hurles her to shore, and rends her on the rockes;
So stood she long 'twixt love and reason tost,
Until despaire (who where it comes rules most)
Wonne her to throw herselfe, to meete with death,
From off the rocke into the flood beneath.
The waves that were above, when as she fell,
For feare flew backe again into their well;
Doubting ensuing times on them would frowne,
That they so rare a beauty help'd to drowne,
Her fall in griefe, did make the streame so rore,
That sullen murmurings filled all the shore.

Into Latin Prose.

THEN the Romans went home to Rome in triumph, and Horatius went at the head of the army, bearing his triple spoils. But as they were drawing near to the Capenian gate, his sister came out to meet him. Now she had been betrothed in marriage to one of the Curiatii, and his cloak, which she had wrought with her own hands, was borne on the shoulders of her brother; and she knew it, and cried out, and wept for him whom she had loved. At the sight of her tears Horatius was so wroth, that he drew his sword, and stabbed his sister to the heart; and he said, "So perish the Roman maiden who shall weep for her country's enemy." But men said that it was a dreadful deed, and they dragged him before the two judges who judged when blood had been shed. For thus said the law:

"The two men shall give judgment on the shedder of blood.

If he shall appeal from their judgment, let the appeal be tried.

If their judgment be confirmed, cover his head.

Hang him with a halter on the accursed tree;

Scourge him either within the sacred limit of the city or without."

So they gave judgment on Horatius, and were going to give him over to be put to death. But he appealed, and the appeal was tried before all the Romans, and they would not condemn him, because he had conquered for them their enemies, and because his father spoke for him, and said, that he judged the maiden to have been lawfully slain. Yet as blood had been shed, which required to be atoned for, the Romans gave a certain sum of money, to offer sacrifices to atone for the pollution of blood. These sacrifices were duly performed ever afterwards by the members of the house of the Horatii.

Translate Sophocles, *Antigone*, v. 403, τοιοῦτον... 436, σωτηρίας.

Into Latin Elegiacs.

Shepherd, I pray thee stay! Where hast thou been?
Or whither go'st thou? Here be woods as green
As any, air likewise as fresh and sweet,
As where smooth Zephyrus plays on the fleet
Face of the curled streams, with flowers as many
As the young spring gives, and as choice as any

Here be all new delights, cool streams and wells,
Arbours o'ergreen with woodbines; caves and dells;
Choose where thou wilt, whilst I sit by and sing,
Or gather rushes to make many a ring
For thy long fingers; tell the tales of love,
How the pale Phœbe, hunting in a grove,
First saw the boy Endymion, from whose eyes
She took eternal fire that never dies;
How she convey'd him softly in a sleep,
His temples bound with poppy, to the steep
Head of old Latmus, where she stops each night,
Gilding the mountain with her brother's light,
To kiss her sweetest.

Into Greek Iambics.

Look, sister, ere the vapour dim thy brain:
Beneath is a wide plain of billowy mist,
As a lake, paving in the morning sky,
With azure waves which burst in silver light,
Some Indian vale. Behold it, rolling on
Under the curdling winds, and islanding
The peak whereon we stand, midway, around,
Encinctured by the dark and blooming forests,
Dim twilight-lawns, and stream-illumined caves,
And wind-enchanted shapes of wandering mist;
And far on high the keen sky-cleaving mountains
From icy spires of sun-like radiance fling
The dawn, as lifted Ocean's dazzling spray,
From some Atlantic islet scattered up,
Spangles the wind with lamp-like water-drops.

Translate TACITUS, *Annals, Book* XVI. *Chap.* 33.

Into Latin Alcaics.

CAPTAIN or Colonel, or Knight in arms,
Whose chance on these defenceless doors may cease,
If deed of honour did thee ever please,
Guard them, and him within protect from harms.

He can requite thee, for he knows the charms
That call fame on such gentle acts as these,
And he can spread thy name o'er lands and seas,
Whatever clime the sun's bright circle warms.

Lift not thy spear against the Muses' bow'r:
The great Emathian conqueror bid spare
The house of Pindarus, when temple and tow'r
Went to the ground: and the repeated air
Of sad Electra's poet had the pow'r
To save the Athenian walls from ruin bare.

Into Greek Prose.

IT hath ben noted by divers, that Homer in Poesie, Aristotle in Philosophy, Demosthenes in Eloquence, and others of the ancients, in other knowledge, do still maintain their primacy, none of them exceeded, some not approached by any in these later ages. And in the number of these is justly ranked also our Thucydides; a workman no less perfect in his work than any of the former; and in whom (I believe with many others) the faculty of writing history is at the highest. For the principal and proper work of history being to instruct, and enable men by the knowledge of actions *past*, to bear themselves prudently in the *present*, and providently towards the *future*, there is not extant any other (merely human) that doth more fully and naturally perform it, than this of my author. It is true, that there be many excellent and profitable histories written since; and in some of them there be inserted very wise discourses both of *manners* and *policy*. But being discourses inserted, and not of the contexture of the narration, they indeed commend the knowledge of the writer, but not the history itself; the nature whereof is merely narrative. In others, there be subtile conjectures at the secret aims and inward cogitations of such as fall under their pen; which is also none of the least virtues in a history, where the conjecture is thoroughly grounded, not forced to serve the purpose of the writer, in adorning his style, or manifesting his subtlety in conjecturing. But these conjectures cannot often be certain, unless withal so evident, that the narration itself may be sufficient to suggest the same also to the reader. But Thucydides is one, who, though he never digress, to read a lecture, moral or political, upon his own text, nor enter into men's hearts, further than the actions themselves evidently guide him, is yet accounted the most polite historiographer that ever writ. The reason whereof I take to be this: He filleth his narrations with that choice of matter, and ordereth them with that judgment, and with such perspicuity and efficacy expresseth himself, that (as Plutarch saith) he maketh his auditor a spectator. For he setteth his reader in the *assemblies of the people* and in the *senates*, at their debating, in the *streets*, at their seditions; and in the *field*, at their battles. So that look how much a man of understanding might have added to his experience, if he had then lived, a beholder of their proceedings, and familiar with the men, and business of the time; so much almost may be profit now, by attentive reading of the same here written. He may from the narrations draw out lessons to himself, and of himself be able to trace the drifts and counsels of the actors to their seat.

Translate VIRGIL, *Georg.* II. vv. 83—108.

Into Latin Hexameters.

Now great Hyperion left his golden throne
That on the dancing waves in glory shone,
For whose declining on the western shore
The orientall hils blacke mantles wore,
And thence apace the gentle twilight fled,
That had from hideous caverns ushered
All drowsie night; who in a carre of jet,
By steeds of iron-gray (which mainely swet
Moist drops on all the world) drawne through the skye,
The helpes of darknesse waited orderly.
First thicke clouds rose from all the liquid plaines:
Then mists from marishes, and grounds whose veynes
Were conduit-pipes to many a christall spring:
From standing pooles and fens were following
Unhealthy fogs: each river, every rill
Sent up their vapours to attend her will.
These pitchy curtains drew 'twixt earth and heaven,
And as night's chariot through the ayre was driven,
Clamour grew dumb, unheard was shepherd's song,
And silence girt the woods; no warbling tongue
Talk'd to the echo: satyres broke their dance,
And all the upper world lay in a trance.

Onely the curled streams soft chidings kept;
And little gales that from the greene leafe swept
Dry summer's dust, in fearefull whisp'rings stirr'd,
As loath to waken any singing bird.

Into Greek Iambics.

Sweet is the breath of morn, her rising sweet,
With charm of earliest birds; pleasant the sun,
When first on this delightful land he spreads
His orient beams, on herb, tree, fruit and flower,
Glist'ring with dew; fragrant the fertile earth
After soft showers; and sweet the coming on
Of grateful ev'ning mild; then silent night
With this her solemn bird, and this fair moon,
And these the gems of heav'n, her starry train:
But neither breath of morn when she ascends
With charm of earliest birds, nor rising sun
On this delightful land, nor herb, fruit, flower,
Glist'ring with dew, nor fragrance after showers,
Nor grateful evening mild, nor silent night
With this her solemn bird, nor walk by moon,
Or glittering starlight, without thee is sweet.

Into Latin Lyrics.

He that loves a rosy cheek,
  Or a coral lip admires,
Or from star-like eyes doth seek
  Fuel to maintain his fires;
As old time makes these decay,
So his flames must waste away.

But a smooth and stedfast mind,
    Gentle thoughts and calm desires,
Hearts with equal love combin'd,
    Kindle never-dying fires.
Where these are not, I despise
Lovely cheeks, or lips, or eyes.

No tears, Celia, now shall win
    My resolv'd heart to return;
I have search'd thy soul within,
    And find nought but pride and scorn:
I have learn'd thy arts, and now
Can disdain as much as thou.
Some pow'r, in my revenge convey
That love to her I cast away.

Translate HERODOTUS, *Book* v. *Chap.* 101.

Into Greek Prose in the style of Herodotus.

THIS Deioces was the first that ruled the Medes in a strict forme, commanding more absolutely than his predecessors had done. For they, following the example of Arbaces, had given to the people so much licence as caused every one to desire the wholesome severitie of a more lordly king. Herein Deioces answered their desire to the full. For he caused them to build for him a stately palace; he tooke unto him a guard, for defence of his person; he seldome gave presence, which also when he did, it was with such austeritie, that no man durst presume to spit or cough in his sight. By these and the like ceremonies he bred in the people an awfull regard, and highly upheld the majestic, which his predecessors had almost letten fall, through neglect of due comportments. In execution of his royall office he did uprightly and severely administer justice, keeping secret spies to informe him of all that was done in the kingdom. He cared not to enlarge the bounds of his dominion, by encroaching upon others; but studied how to govern well his own.

Into Latin Prose.

This resolution of Nicias, though it cannot be commended, (for it is the part of an honest and valiant man to do what reason willeth, not what opinion expecteth; and to measure honour or dishonour by the assurance of his well-informed conscience, rather than the malicious report and censure of others,) yet it may be excused; since he had before his eyes the injustice of his people, and had well understood that a wicked sentence is infinitely worse than a wicked fact, as being held a president and pattern whereby oppression beginning upon one, is extended as warrantable upon all. Therefore his feare of wrongfull condemnation was such, as a constant man could not easily have over-mastered; but when afterwards the army having no other expectation of safety than the faint hope of a secret flight; he was so terrefied with an eclipse of the moon, happening when they were about to dislodge, that he would not consent to have the camp break up till seven and twenty dayes were past. His timerousnesse was even as foolish and ridiculous, as the issue of it was lamentable. For he should not have thought that the power of the Heavens, and the course of nature would be as unjust as his Athenians, or might pretend lesse evill to the slothfull, than to such as did their best. Neither doe I think that any astrologer can alledge this eclipse, as either a cause or prognostication of that armie's destruction, otherwise than as the folly of men did, by application, turne it to their owne confusion. Had C. Cassius the Roman, he who slew Julius Cæsar, imitated this superstition of Nicias, he had surely found the same fortune in a case very like. But when, hee ,retyring, the broken remainder of Crassus his army defeated by the Parthian archers, was advised, upon such an accident as this, to continue where he then was, till the sunne were past the signe of Scorpio; he made answer that he stood not in such feare of Scorpio, as of Sagittarius. So adventuring rather to abide the frowning of the heavens, than the nearer danger of enemies upon earth, he made such a safe and honourable retreat, as did both show his noble resolution, and give a faire example to that good rule.

Translate ÆSCHYLUS, *Agamemnon* (*ed.* Scholefield), v. 619, εὔφημον ἦμαρ ... *to* v. 663, κλύων.

Into Greek Iambics.

MILD, affable, and easy of access
He was; but with a due reservedness:
So that the passage to his favours lay
Not common to all comers; nor yet was
So narrow, but it gave a gentle way
To such as fitly might, or ought to pass.
Nor sold he smoke; nor took he up to-day
Commodities of men's attendances,
And of their hopes; to pay them with delay,
And entertain them with fair promises.

But as a man that lov'd no great commerce
With bus'ness and with noise, he ever flies
That maze of many ways, which might disperse
Him into other men's uncertainties:
And with a quiet calm sincerity,
H' effects his undertakings really.
His tongue and heart did not turn backs; but went
One way, and kept one course with what he meant.
He us'd no mark at all, but ever ware
His honest inclination open-faced:
The friendships that he vow'd most constant were,
And with great judgment and discretion plac'd

Into Latin Hexameters.

In costly sheen, and gaudy cloak array'd,
But all afoot, the light-limb'd Matadore
Stands in the centre, eager to invade
The lord of lowing herds; but not before
The ground, with cautious tread, is travers'd o'er,
Lest aught unseen should lurk to thwart his speed:
His arms a dart, he fights aloof, nor more
Can man achieve without the friendly steed—
Alas! too oft condemn'd for him to bear and bleed.

Thrice sounds the clarion: lo! the signal falls,
The den expands, and Expectation mute
Gapes round the silent circle's peopled walls.
Bounds with one lashing spring the mighty brute,
And, wildly staring, spurns, with sounding foot,
The sand, nor blindly rushes on his foe:
Here, there, he points his threatening front, to suit
His first attack, wide waving to and fro
His angry tail; red rolls his eye's dilated glow.

Sudden he stops; his eye is fix'd: away,
Away, thou heedless boy! prepare the spear;
Now is thy time, to perish or display
The skill that yet may check his mad career.
With well-timed croupe the nimble coursers veer;
On foams the bull, but not unscath'd he goes;
Streams from his flank the crimson torrent clear:
He flies, he wheels, distracted with his throes;
Dart follows dart: lance, lance; loud bellowings speak
    his woes.

Translate HORACE, *Book* II. *Ode* 1.

For Latin Lyrics.

On Linden, when the sun was low,
All bloodless lay th' untrodden snow,
And dark as winter was the flow
Of Iser, rolling rapidly.

But Linden saw another sight,
When the drum beat, at dead of night,
Commanding fires of death to light
The darkness of her scenery.

By torch and trumpet fast array'd
Each horseman drew his battle-blade,
And furious every charger neigh'd
To join the dreadful revelry.

Then shook the hills with thunder riven,
Then rush'd the steed to battle driven,
And louder than the bolts of heaven,
Far flash'd the red artillery.

But redder yet that light shall glow
On Linden's hills of stained snow,
And bloodier yet the torrent flow
Of Iser, rolling rapidly.

'Tis morn, but scarce yon level sun
Can pierce the war-clouds, rolling dun,
Where furious Frank and fiery Hun
Shout in their sulph'rous canopy.

The combat deepens. On ye brave,
Who rush to glory, or the grave!
Wave Munich! all thy banners wave!
And charge with all thy chivalry!

Few, few, shall part where many meet!
The snow shall be their winding-sheet,
And every turf beneath their feet
Shall be a soldier's sepulchre.

Translate THUCYDIDES, *Book* IV. *Chaps.* 33—35.

Into Greek Prose.

MEN of Peloponnesus, as for your country, how by valour it hath ever retained her liberty; and that being Dorians, you are now to fight against Ionians, of whom you were ever wont to get the victory, let it suffice that I have touched it thus briefly. But in what manner I intend to charge, that I am now to inform you of; lest the venturing by few at once, and not altogether, should seem to proceed from weakness, and so dishearten you. I do conjecture that it was in contempt of us, and as not expecting to be fought withal, that the enemy both came up to this place, and that they have now betaken themselves carelessly, and out of order, to view the country. But he that best observing such errors in his enemies, shall also to his strength give the onset, not always openly, and in ranged battle, but as is best for his present advantage, shall for the most part attain his purpose. And these wiles carry with them the greatest glory of all, by which deceiving most the enemy, a man doth most benefit his friends. Therefore, whilst they are secure without preparation, and intend, for ought I see, to steal away, rather than to stay, I say, in this their looseness of resolution, and before they put their minds in order, I for my part, with those I have chosen, will, if I can, before they get away, fall in upon the midst of their army, running. And you Clearidas, afterwards, as soon as you see me to have charged and (as it is probable) to have put them into a fright, take those that are with you, both Amphipolitans, and all the rest of the confederates, and setting open the gates, run out upon them, and with all possible speed come up to a stroke of hand (for there is great hope this way to terrify them, seeing they which come after are ever of more terror to the enemy than those that are already present, and in fight). And be valiant, as is likely you should that are a Spartan; and you confederates follow manfully, and believe that the parts of a good soldier are willingness, sense of shame, and obedience to his leaders; and that this day you shall either gain yourselves liberty by your valour, and to be called confederates of the Lacedæmonians, or else not only to serve the Athenians yourselves, and at the best, if you be not led captives, nor put to death, to be in greater servitude than before, but also to be the hinderers of the liberty of the rest of the Græcians. But be not you cowards, seeing how great a matter is at stake; and I for my part will make it appear that I am not more ready to persuade another, than to put myself into action.

Translate TACITUS, *Annals, Book* xv. *Chaps.* 63, 64

Into Latin Prose.

IN the arduous task which Claudius had undertaken, of restoring the empire to its ancient splendour, it was first necessary to revive among his troops a sense of order and obedience. With the authority of a veteran commander, he represented to them, that the relaxation of discipline had introduced a long train of disorders, the effects of which were at length experienced by the soldiers themselves; that a people ruined by oppression, and indolent from despair, could no longer supply a numerous army with the means of luxury, or even of subsistence; that the danger of each individual had increased with the despotism of the military order, since princes who tremble on the throne, will guard their safety by the instant sacrifice of every obnoxious subject. The emperor expatiated on the mischiefs of a lawless caprice, which the soldiers could only gratify at the expense of their own blood; as their seditious elections had so frequently been followed by civil wars, which consumed the flower of the legions either in the field of battle, or in the cruel abuse of victory. He painted, in the most lively colours, the exhausted state of the treasury, the desolation of the provinces, the disgrace of the Roman name, and the insolent triumph of rapacious barbarians. It was against those barbarians, he declared, that he intended to point the first effort of their arms. Tetricus might reign for a while over the West, and even Zenobia might preserve the dominion of the East. These usurpers were his perpetual adversaries; nor could he think of indulging any private resentment till he had saved an empire, whose impending ruin would, unless it was timely prevented, crush both the army and the people.

Translate LUCRETIUS, *Book* III. v. 1058. *Tu vero dubitabis* ... end.

Into Latin Hexameters.

By ceaseless action all that is subsists,
Constant rotation of th' unwearied wheel,
That Nature rides upon, maintains her health,
Her beauty, her fertility. She dreads
An instant's pause, and lives but while she moves—
Its own revolvency upholds the world.
Winds from all quarters agitate the air,
And fit the liquid element for use,
Else noxious; oceans, rivers, lakes, and streams,
All feel the fresh'ning impulse, and are cleans'd
By restless undulation: ev'n the oak
Thrives by the rude concussion of the storm:
He seems indeed indignant, and to feel
Th' impression of the blast with proud disdain,
Frowning, as if in his unconscious arm
He held the thunder: but the monarch owes
His firm stability to what he scorns,
More fix'd below, the more disturb'd above.

The law, by which all creatures else are bound,
Binds man, the lord of all—himself derives
No mean advantage from a kindred cause,
From strenuous toil his hours of sweetest ease.

Into Latin Prose.

THE Roman sceptre, the reward of his crimes, was held by Andronicus about three years and a half, as the guardian or sovereign of the empire. His government exhibited a singular contrast of vice and virtue. When he listened to his passions, he was the scourge, when he consulted his reason, the father, of his people. In the exercise of private justice, he was equitable and rigorous; a shameful and pernicious venality was abolished, and the offices were filled with the most deserving candidates, by a prince who had sense to choose, and severity to punish. He prohibited the inhuman practice of pillaging the goods and persons of shipwrecked mariners; the provinces, so long the objects of oppression or neglect, revived in prosperity and plenty; and millions applauded the distant blessings of his reign, while he was cursed by the witnesses of his daily cruelties. The ancient proverb, that blood-thirsty is the man who returns from banishment to power, had been applied with too much truth to Marius and Tiberius; and was now verified for the third time in the life of Andronicus. His memory was stored with a black list of the enemies and rivals who had traduced his merit, opposed his greatness, or insulted his misfortunes; and the only comfort of his exile was the sacred hope and promise of revenge.

Into Greek Iambics.

✝ I NEVER looked that he should live so long.
He was a man of that unsleeping spirit,
He seemed to live by miracle: his food
Was glory, which was poison to his mind,
And peril to his body. He was one
Of many thousand such, that die betimes,
Whose story is a fragment, known to few.
Then comes the man that has the luck to live,
And he's a prodigy. Compute the chances,
And deem there's ne'er a one in dangerous times
Who wins the race of glory, but than him
A thousand men more gloriously endowed
Have fallen upon the course: a thousand others
Have had their fortunes foundered by a chance,
Whilst lighter barks pushed by them: to whom add
A smaller tally, of the singular few,
Who, gifted with predominating powers,
Bear yet a temperate will, and keep the peace. ✝

Into Latin Lyrics, or Greek Anapæsts.

SING his praises that doth keep
   Our flocks from harm,
Pan, the father of our sheep;
   And arm in arm
Tread we softly in a round,
While the hollow neighb'ring ground
Fills the music with her sound.

Pan, oh, great god Pan, to thee
   Thus do we sing:

Thou that keep'st us chaste and free,
  As the young spring,
Ever be thy honour spoke,
From that place the morn is broke,
To that place day doth unyoke!

Into Latin Elegiacs.

In glowing youth he stood beside
His native stream, and saw it glide
Showing each gem beneath its tide,
Calm as though nought could break its rest,
Reflecting heaven on its breast,
And seeming, in its flow to be
Like candour, peace, and piety.

When life began in brilliant dream,
His heart was like his native stream;
The wave-shrined gems could scarcely seem
Less hidden than each wish it knew;
Its life flowed on as calmly too;
And heaven shielded it from sin,
To see itself reflected in.

He stood beside that stream again,
When years had fled in strife and pain;
He looked for its calm course in vain,—
For storms profaned its peaceful flow,
And clouds o'erhung its crystal brow:—
And turning there, he sigh'd to deem
His heart still like his native stream.

Translate Euripides, *Hecuba*, v.774, οὐκ εστιν ...
    833, κακῶς ἀεί.

Into Greek Iambics.

✢   Nay, said I not—
And if I said it not, I say it now—
I'll follow thee through sunshine and through storm;
I will be with thee in thy weal and woe,
In thy afflictions, should they fall upon thee,
In thy temptations when bad men beset thee,
In all the perils which must now press round thee,
And should they crush thee, in the hour of death.
If thy ambition, late aroused was that
Which push'd thee on this perilous adventure,
Then *I* will be ambitious too—if not,
And it was thy ill fortune drove thee to it,
Then I will be unfortunate no less.
I will resemble thee in that and all things
Wherein a woman may: grave will I be
And thoughtful, for already is it gone—
The boon that nature gave me at my birth,
My own original gaiety of heart.   ✢

Translate Demosthenes, περὶ στεφάνου, *from* επειδὴ τοίνυν, p. 269, *to* αναμνήσω, p. 271.

For Greek Prose.

Surely it is great injustice to impute the mischiefe contrived against worthy men, to their own proud carriage, or some other ill deserving. For though it often happen, that small vices do serve to counterpoise great vertues; (the sense of evill being more quick and lasting than of good) yet he shall bewray a very foolish malice, that, wanting other testimonie, will thinke it a part of wisedome, to finde good reason of the evills done to vertuous men, which oftentimes have no other cause than vertue itselfe. Eumenes, among many excellent qualities, was noted to be of singular courtesie, of a very sweet conversation among his friends, and carefull by all gentle meanes to winne their love, that seemed to beare him any secret ill affection. It was his meere vertue that overthrew him, which even they that sought his life acknowledged.

Translate TACITUS, *Annal.* I. 42, 43.

Into Latin Prose.

BEING brought to Rome, the people as to a solemn spectacle were call'd together, the emperor's guard stood in arms. In order came first, the king's servants, bearing his trophies won in other wars: next, his brothers, wife, and daughter, last himself. The behaviour of others through fear, was low and degenerate; he only neither in countenance, word, or action, submissive, standing at the tribunal of Claudius, briefly spake to this purpose. "If my mind, Cæsar, had been as moderate in the height of fortune, as my birth and dignity was eminent, I might have come a friend rather than a captive into this city. Nor couldest thou have disliked him for a confederate, so noble of descent, and ruling so many nations. My present estate to me disgraceful, to thee is glorious. I had riches, horses, arms, and men; nor wonder then if I contended, not to lose them; but if by fate, yours only must be empire, then of necessity ours among the rest must be subjection. If I sooner had been brought to yield, my misfortune had been less notorious, your conquest had been less renowned; and in your severest determining of me, both will be soon forgotten. But if you grant that I shall live, by me will live to you for ever that praise which is so near divine, the clemency of a conqueror." Cæsar, moved at such a spectacle of fortune, but especially at the nobleness of his bearing it, gave him pardon, and to all the rest.

Into Latin or Greek Elegiacs.

TELL me not, sweet, I am unkind,
    That from the nunnery
Of thy chaste breast and quiet mind
    To war and arms I fly.
True: a new mistress now I chase
    The first foe in the field;
And with a stronger faith embrace
    A sword, a horse, a shield.
Yet this inconstancy is such,
    As you too shall adore;
I could not love thee, dear, so much,
    Lov'd I not honour more.

Into Latin Hexameters.

Lo! the green serpent from his dark abode,
Which ev'n imagination fears to tread,
At noon forth issuing, gathers up his train
In orbs immense: then darting out anew,
Seeks the refreshing fount, by which diffus'd
He throws his folds: and while with threat'ning tongue
And deathful jaws erect the monster curls
His flaming crest, all other thirst appall'd,

Or shiv'ring flies, or check'd at distance stands,
Nor dares approach. But still more direful he,
The small close-lurking minister of fate,
Whose high concocted venom through the veins
A rapid lightning darts, arresting swift
The vital current. Form'd to humble man,
This child of vengeful nature; there sublim'd
To fearless lust of blood, the savage race
Roam, licens'd by the shading hour of guilt
And foul misdeed, when the pure day has shut
His sacred eye. The tyger, darting fierce,
Impetuous on the prey his glance has doom'd;
The lively shining leopard speckled o'er
With many a spot, the beauty of the waste;
And, scorning all the taming arts of man,
The keen hyena, fellest of the fell.
These rushing from the inhospitable woods
Of Mauritania, or the tufted isles
That verdant rise amid the Lybian wild,
Innumerous glare around their shaggy king
Majestic, stalking o'er the printed sand:
And with imperious and repeated roars
Demand their fated food. The fearful flocks
Crowd near the guardian swain; the nobler herds,
Where round their lordly bull in rural ease
They ruminating lie, with horror hear
The coming rage. Th' awaken'd village starts,
And to her fluttering breast the mother strains
Her thoughtless infant. From the pirate's den
Or stern Morocco's tyrant fang escap'd,
The wretch half wishes for his bonds again;
While uproar all, the wilderness resounds
From Atlas eastward to the frighted Nile.

Translate SOPHOCLES, *Œdipus Coloneus*, 613, ὦ φίλτατ'... 634, ψεύσουσί με.

Into Greek Iambics.

I DO believe you innocent, a good man,
And Heav'n forgive that naughty thing that wrong'd me!
Why look ye wild, my friends? why stare ye on me?
I charge ye, as ye're men, my men, my lovers,
As ye are honest faithful men, fair soldiers,
Let down your anger! Is not this our sovereign?
The head of mercy and of law? Who dares then
But rebels, scorning law, appear thus violent?
Is this a place for swords, for threat'ning fires?
The rev'rence of this house dares any touch,
But with obedient knees, and pious duties?
Are we not all his subjects, all sworn to him?
Has he not pow'r to punish our offences,
And don't we daily fall into 'em? Assure yourselves
I did offend, and highly, grievously;
This good sweet prince I offended, my life forfeited,
Which yet his mercy, and his old love met with,
And only let me feel his light rod this way.
Ye are to thank him for your general,
Pray for his life and fortune, sweat your bloods for him.
Ye are offenders too, daily offenders;
Proud insolencies dwell in your hearts, and ye do 'em,
Do 'em against his peace, his law, his person;
Ye see he only sorrows for your sins,
And where his pow'r might persecute, forgives ye.

For a Greek or Latin Epigram.

While on the cliff with calm delight she kneels,
And the blue vales a thousand joys recall,
See to the last, last verge her infant steals!
O fly—yet stir not, speak not, lest it fall.
Far better taught, she lays her bosom bare,
And the fond boy springs back to nestle there.

Translate Thucydides, *Book* III. *Chaps.* 83, 84.

Into Greek Prose.

These conclusions are so natural and obvious, that they have not escaped even the poets in their descriptions of the felicity, attending the golden age, or the reign of Saturn. The seasons in that first period of nature were so temperate, if we credit these agreeable fictions, that there was no necessity for men to provide themselves with clothes and houses, as a security against the violence of heat and cold: the rivers flowed with wine and milk: the oaks yielded honey, and nature spontaneously produced her greatest delicacies. Nor were these the chief advantages of that happy age. Tempests were not alone removed from nature; but those more furious tempests were unknown to human breasts, which now cause such uproar, and engender such confusion. Avarice, ambition, cruelty, selfishness, were never heard of; cordial affection, compassion, sympathy, were the only movements with which the mind was yet acquainted. Even the punctilious distinction of *mine* and *thine* was banished from among that happy race of mortals, and carried with it the very notion of property and obligation, justice and injustice.

Translate HORACE, *Book* IV. *Ode* 9.

Into Latin Lyrics.

He that of such a height hath built his mind,
And rear'd the dwelling of his thoughts so strong,
As neither fear nor hope can shake the frame
Of his resolv'd pow'rs; nor all the wind
Of vanity or malice pierce to wrong
His settled peace, or to disturb the same:
What a fair seat hath he, from whence he may
The boundless wastes and wilds of man survey!
And with how free an eye doth he look down
Upon these lower regions of turmoil,
Where all the storms of passions mainly beat
Of flesh and blood; where honour, pow'r, renown,
Are only gay afflictions, golden toil;
Where greatness stands upon as feeble feet
As frailty doth; and only great doth seem
To little minds, who do it so esteem.

Translate LIVY, *Book* v. *Chap.* 37.

Into Latin Prose.

The perpetual revolutions of the throne had so perfectly erased every notion of hereditary right, that the family of an unfortunate emperor was incapable of exciting the jealousy of his successors. The children of Tacitus and Florianus were permitted to descend into a private station, and to mingle with the general mass of the people. Their poverty indeed became an additional safeguard to their innocence. When Tacitus was elected by the senate, he resigned his ample patrimony to the public service; an act of generosity, specious in appearance, but which evidently disclosed his intention of transmitting the empire to his descendants. The only consolation of their fallen state, was the remembrance of transient greatness, and a distant hope, the child of a flattering prophecy, that, at the end of a thousand years, a monarch of the race of Tacitus should arise, the protector of the senate, the restorer of Rome, and the conqueror of the whole earth.

Into Latin Hexameters.

Now, by the cool declining year condens'd,
Descend the copious exhalations check'd
As up the middle sky unseen they stole,
And roll the doubling fogs around the hill.
No more the mountain, horrid, vast, sublime,
Who pours a sweep of rivers from his sides,
And high between contending kingdoms rears
The rocky long division, fills the view
With great variety; but in a night
Of gath'ring vapour from the baffled sense
Sinks dark and dreary; thence expanding far
The huge dusk gradual swallows up the plain:
Vanish the woods; the dim-seen river seems
Sullen and slow to roll the misty wave.
Ev'n in the height of noon oppress'd the sun
Sheds weak and blunt his wide-refracted ray,
Whence glaring oft with many a broaden'd orb
He frights the nations. Indistinct on earth,
Seen through the turbid air, beyond the life

Objects appear, and wilder'd o'er the waste
The shepherd stalks gigantic: till at last
Wreath'd dun around in deeper circles still
Successive closing, sits the general fog
Unbounded o'er the world, and mingling thick,
A formless gray confusion covers all.

Into Greek Prose.

AMONG all the nations of antiquity, the structure of their vessels was extremely rude, and their method of working them very defective. They were unacquainted with several principles and operations in navigation, which are now considered as the first elements on which that science is founded. Though that property of the magnet, by which it attracts iron, was well known to the ancients, its more important and amazing virtue, of pointing to the poles, had entirely escaped their observation. Destitute of this faithful guide, which now conducts the pilot with so much certainty in the unbounded ocean, during the darkness of night, or when the heavens are covered with clouds, the ancients had no other method of regulating their course than by observing the sun and stars. Their navigation was of cousequence uncertain, and timid. They durst seldom quit sight of land, but crept along the coast, exposed to all the dangers, and retarded by all the obstructions, unavoidable in holding such an awkward course. An incredible length of time was requisite for performing voyages, which are now finished in a short space. Even in the mildest climates, and in seas the least tempestuous, it was only during the summer months that the ancients ventured out of their harbours. The remainder of the year was lost in inactivity.

It would have been deemed most inconsiderate rashness to have braved the fury of the winds and waves during winter.

Into Latin Elegiacs.

Not all the ointments brought from Delos' isle;
Nor from the confines of seven-headed Nyle:
Nor that brought whence Phœnicians have abodes;
Nor Cyprus' wilde vine-flowers; nor that of Rhodes;
Nor roses-oyle from Naples, Capua,
Saffron confected in Cilecia;
Nor that of quinces, nor of marioram,
That ever from the isle of Coös came:
Nor these, nor any else, though ne'er so rare,
Could with this place for sweetest smels compare.
There stood the elme, whose shade so mildly dym
Doth nourish all that groweth under him.
Cipresses, that like piramides runne topping,
And hurt the least of any by their dropping.
The alder, whose fat shadow nourisheth,
Each plant set neere to him long flowrisheth.
The heavie-headed plane-tree, by whose shade
The grasse growes thickest, men are fresher made.
The oake, that best endures the thunder shocks:
The everlasting ebene, cedar, boxe;
The olive that in wainscot never cleaves:
The amorous vine which in the elme still weaves.

Translate CICERO *pro Cluentio, Chaps.* 18, 19.

Into Latin Prose.

I HAVE sometimes been inclined to think, that interruptions in the periods of learning, were they not attended with such a destruction of ancient books, and the records of history, would be rather favourable to the arts and sciences, by breaking the progress of authority, and dethroning the tyrannical usurpers over human reason. In this particular, they have the same influence, as interruptions in political governments and societies. Consider the blind submission of the ancient philosophers to the several masters in each school, and you will be convinced that little good could be expected from an hundred centuries of such a servile philosophy. Even the Eclectics, who arose about the age of Augustus, notwithstanding their professing to choose freely what pleased them from every different sect, were yet, in the main, as slavish and dependent as any of their brethren; since they sought for truth, not in nature, but in the several schools; where they supposed she must necessarily be found, though not united in a body, yet dispersed in parts. Upon the revival of learning, those sects of Stoics and Epicureans, Platonists and Pythagoricians, could never regain any credit or authority; and at the same time, by the example of their fall, kept men from submitting with such blind deference to those new sects which have attempted to gain an ascendant over them.

Into Greek Iambics.

AWFUL Sufferer,
To thee unwilling, most unwillingly
I come, by the great Father's will driven down,
To execute a doom of new revenge.

Alas! I pity thee, and hate myself
That I can do no more: aye from thy sight
Returning, for a season, heaven seems hell,
So thy worn form pursues me night and day,
Smiling reproach. Wise art thou, firm and good,
But vainly would'st stand forth alone in strife
Against the Omnipotent: as yon clear lamps,
That measure and divide the weary years
From which there is no refuge, long have taught,
And long must teach. Even now thy torturer arms
With the strange might of unimagined pains
The powers who scheme slow agonies in hell,
And my commission is to lead them here,
Or what more subtle, foul, or savage fiends
People the abyss, and leave them to their task.
Be it not so! there is a secret known
To thee, and to none else of living things,
Which may transfer the sceptre of wide heaven,
The fear of which perplexes the Supreme:
Clothe it in words, and bid it clasp his throne
In intercession; bend thy soul in prayer,
And, like a suppliant in some gorgeous fane,
Let the will kneel within thy haughty heart:
For benefits and meek submission tame
The fiercest and the mightiest.

Into Latin Lyrics.

O HOW much more doth beauty beauteous seem,
By that sweet ornament which truth doth give!
The rose looks fair, but fairer we it deem
For that sweet odour which doth in it live:
The canker-blooms have full as deep a dye

As the perfumed tincture of the roses,
Hang on such thorns, and play as wantonly
When summer's breath their masked buds discloses:
But, for their virtue only is their show,
They live unwoo'd, and unrespected fade;
Die to themselves. Sweet roses do not so;
Of their sweet deaths are sweetest odours made:
And so of you, beauteous and lovely youth,
When that shall fade, by verse distills your truth.

Translate HOMER, *Iliad* XIV. vv. 153—186.

Into Greek or Latin Hexameters.

THERE lies a vale in Ida, lovelier
Than all the valleys of Ionian hills.
The swimming vapour slopes athwart the glen,
Puts forth an arm, and creeps from pine to pine,
And loiters, slowly drawn. On either hand
The lawns and meadow-ledges midway down
Hang rich in flowers, and far below them roars
The long brook falling through the clov'n ravine
In cataract after cataract to the sea.
Behind the valley topmast Gargarus
Stands up and takes the morning: but in front
The gorges, opening wide apart, reveal
Troas and Ilion's column'd citadel,
The crown of Troas.
     Hither came at noon
Mournful Œnone, wandering forlorn
Of Paris, once her playmate on the hills.
Her cheek had lost the rose, and round her neck

Floated her hair or seem'd to float in rest.
She, leaning on a fragment twined with vine,
Sang to the stillness, till the mountain-shade
Sloped downward to her seat from the upper cliff.

Translate LUCRETIUS, *Book* I. v. 272...*principio,* to
v. 298, *corpore qui sunt.*

Into Latin Hexameters.

    As Tavy creepes upon
The westerne vales of fertile Albion,
Here dashes roughly on an aged rocke,
That his extended passage doth up locke;
There intricately 'mongst the woods doth wander,
Losing himself in many a wry meander:
Here amorously bent, clips some faire meade;
And then disperst in rills, doth measures treade
Upon her bosom 'mongst her flow'ry rankes;
There in another place beares downe the bankes
Of some day-labouring wretch: heere meets a rill,
And with their forces joynde cut out a mill
Into an iland, then in jocund guise
Survayes his conquest, lauds his enterprise:
Here digs a cave at some high mountaine's foote:
There undermines an oak, tears up his roote:
Thence rushing to some country farme at hand,
'Breakes o'er the yeoman's mounds, sweepes from his land
His harvest hope of wheate, of rye, or pease:
And makes that channell which was shepheard's lease:
Here, as our wicked age doth sacriledge,
Helpes downe an abbey, then a naturall bridge,

By creeping underground he frameth out,
As who should say he eyther went about
To right the wrong he did, or hid his face,
For having done a deed so vild and base:
So ranne this river on, and did bestirre
Himselfe, to finde his fellow-traveller.

Into Latin Alçaics.

☦ Not seldom, clad in radiant vest,
Deceitfully goes forth the morn:
Not seldom evening in the west
    Sinks smilingly forsworn.

The smoothest seas will sometimes prove
To the confiding bark untrue:
And if she trusts the stars above,
    They can be treacherous too.

The umbrageous oak, in pomp outspread,
Full oft, when storms the welkin rend,
Draws lightning down upon the head
    It promised to defend. ☦

But thou art true, Incarnate Lord,
Who didst vouchsafe for man to die;
Thy smile is sure, thy plighted word
    No change can falsify. ☦

Into Latin Elegiacs.

Under the hollow hanging of this hill
There was a cave, cut out by nature's skill;
Or else it seem'd the mount did open 's brest,
That all might see what thoughts be there possest.

Whose gloomy entrance was environ'd round
With shrubs that cloy ill husband's meadow ground:
The thicke-growne hawthorne and the binding bryer,
The holly that out-dares cold winter's ire:
Who all intwinde, each limbe with limbe did deale,
That scarce a glympse of light could inward steale.
An uncouth place, fit for an uncouth minde,
That is as heavy as that cave is blinde;
Here liv'd a man his hoary haires call'd olde,
Upon whose front time many yeares had tolde.
Who, since dame Nature in him feeble grew,
And he unapt to give the world aught new,
The secret power of hearbes, that grow on molde,
Sought aught, to cherish, and relieve the olde.

Into Greek Prose.

THE bridge finished, and the armie brought neere to the sea-side, Xerxes took a view of all his troupes, assembled in the plain of Abidus, being carried up, and seated on a place over-topping the land round about it, and the sea adjoyning: and after he had gloried in his owne happinesse, to behold and command so many nations, and so powerfull an armie and fleet, he suddenly (notwithstanding) burst out into teares, moved with this contemplation, that in one hundred years there should not any one survive of that marvellous multitude; the cause of which sudden change of passion when he uttered to Artabanus his uncle, Artabanus spake to the king to this effect: That which is more lamentable than the dissolution of this great troupe within that number of yeares by the king remembered, is, that the life itselfe which we enjoy is yet more miserable than the end thereof; for in those few dayes given us in this world there is no man among all these, nor elsewhere, that ever found himselfe so accompanied with happinesse, but that he oftentimes pleased himself better with the desire and hope of death, than of living; the incident calamities, diseases, and sorrowes whereto mankinde is subject, being so many and inevitable, that the shortest life doth oftentimes appear unto us overlong; to avoid all which, there is neither refuge nor rest, but in desired death alone.

Into Latin Prose.

THE memory of Elizabeth is still adored in England. The historians of that kingdom, after celebrating her love of her people; her sagacity in discerning their true interest; her steadiness in pursuing it; her wisdom in the choice of her ministers; the glory she acquired by arms; the tranquillity she secured to her subjects; and the increase of fame, of riches, and of commerce, which were the fruits of all these, justly rank her among the most illustrious princes. Even the defects in her character, they observe, were not of a kind pernicious to her people. Her excessive frugality was not accompanied with the love of hoarding; and though it prevented some great undertakings, and rendered the success of others incomplete, it introduced œconomy into her administration, and exempted the nation from many burdens, which a monarch more profuse, or more enterprising, must have imposed. Her slowness in rewarding her servants sometimes discouraged useful merit; but it prevented the undeserving from acquiring power and wealth, to which they had no title. Her extreme jealousy of those princes who pretended to dispute her right to the crown, led her to take such precautions as tended no less to the public safety than to her own; and to court the affections of her people, as the firmest support of her throne. Such is the picture which the English draw of this great queen.

Translate SOPHOCLES, *Ajax, from* v. 425, αἰαῖ ... *to* v. 475, λόγου.

Into Greek Iambics.

It must be—
And yet it moves me, Romans! it confounds
The counsels of my firm philosophy,
That Ruin's merciless ploughshare must pass o'er,
And barren salt be sown on yon proud city,
As on our olive-crowned hill we stand,
Where Kedron at our feet its scanty waters
Distils from stone to stone with gentle motion,
As through a valley sacred to sweet peace.
How boldly doth it front us! how majestically!
Like a luxurious vineyard, the hill side
Is hung with marble fabrics, line o'er line,
Terrace o'er terrace, nearer still and nearer
To the blue heavens. Here bright and sumptuous palaces,
With cool and verdant gardens interspersed;
There towers of war that frown in massy strength;
While over all hangs the rich purple eve,
As conscious of its being her last farewell
Of light and glory to that fated city.
And, as our clouds of battle dust and smoke
Are melted into air, behold the temple,
In undisturb'd and lone serenity
Finding itself a solemn sanctuary

In the profound of heaven! It stands before us,
A mount of snow fretted with golden pinnacles!
The very sun, as though he worshipp'd there,
Lingers upon the gilded cedar-roofs;
And down the long and branching porticoes,
On every flowery sculptured capital,
Glitters the homage of his parting beams.
By Hercules! the sight might almost win
The offended majesty of Rome to mercy.

Translate into Latin Alcaics.

THE soote season, that bud and bloom forth brings,
With green hath clad the hill and eke the vale:
The nightingale with feathers new she sings;
The turtle to her mate hath told her tale:
Summer is come, for every spray now springs;
The hart hath hung his old head on the pale;
The buck in brake his winter coat he flings;
The fishes flete with new-repaired scale;
The adder all her slough away she slings;
The swift swallow pursueth the flies smale;
The busy bee her honey now she mings:
Winter is worn that was the flowers' bale:
And thus I see among these pleasant things
Each care decays, and yet my sorrow springs.

Into Latin Elegiacs.

AND in the midst of all a fountain stood,
Of richest substance that on earth might be,
So pure and shiny, that the silver flood
Through every channel running one might see;

Most goodly it with pure imagery
Was overwrought, and shapes of naked boys,
Of which some seem'd with lively jollity
To fly about, playing their wanton toys,
While others did themselves embathe in liquid joys.

And over all, of purest gold was spread
A trail of ivy in his native hue:
For the rich metal was so coloured,
That wight, who did not well advised it view,
Would surely deem it to be ivy true:
Low his lascivious arms adown did creep,
That themselves dipping in the silver dew,
Their fleecy flowers they tenderly did steep,
Which drops of chrystal seem'd for wantonness to weep.

Infinite streams continually did well
Out of this fountain, sweet and fair to see,
The which into an ample laver fell,
And shortly grew to so great quantity,
That like a little lake it seem'd to be;
Whose depth exceeded not three cubits height,
And through the waves one might the bottom see,
All paved beneath with jasper shining bright,
That seem'd the fountain in that sea did sail upright.

Translate THUCYDIDES, *Book* I. *Chaps.* 32, 33.

Into Greek Prose.

LET us see what powerful aid our enemies are expecting; what confederates they are stirring up against us. The Megareans, who left their alliance for ours; the Megareans, whom we defended against the Corinthians, and whose walls we constructed at our own expense from Megara to Nisæa. Is it on the constancy or on the gratitude of this people that Lacedæmon in her wisdom so confidently relies? No sooner had we landed in Euboea than intelligence was brought us that the Peloponesians were about to make an incursion into Attica, that the Athenian garrison was murdered by the Megareans, who already had formed a junction with the Corinthians, Sicyonians, and Epidaurians. We sailed homeward, and discomfited the Peloponesians; returned, and reduced Euboea. A truce for thirty years was granted to Lacedæmon, restoring to her Nisæa, Calchis, Pegæ, and Trœzene. Five years afterwards a war broke out between the Samians and Miletus. Justice and our treaties obliged us to rescue that faithful and unfortunate city from the two-fold calamity that impended over her. Many of the Samians were as earnest in imploring our assistance as the Milesians were: for, whatever might be the event of the war, they were sure of being reduced to subjection; if conquered, by a wronged and exasperated enemy; if conquerors, by the king. A rapacious and insolent oligarchy saw no other means of retaining its usurped authority, than by extending it with rigour, and were conscious that it must fall from under them unless the sceptre propt it. Honest men will never seek such aid, and free men will never endure such.

⁎ In the late brief war, the greater part of you here present have won immortal glory: and let us not believe that those who fell from your ranks in battle are yet insensible to the admiration and the gratitude of their countrymen. No one among us, whatever services he may have rendered to Athens, has received such praises, such benedictions, such imperishable rewards as they have. Happy men! they are beyond the reach of calumny and reverses. There is only one sad reflection resting with them: they can serve their country no more. How high was the value of their lives! they knew it, and bartered them for renown. We, in this war, unjustly waged against us, shall be exposed to fewer dangers, but more privations. In the endurance of these our manliness will be put severely to the proof, and virtues which have not been called forth in fifty years, virtues which our enemies seem to have forgotten that we possess, must again come into action, as if under the eyes of a Themistocles and an Aristides. We have all done much; but we have all done less than we can do, ought to do, and will do.

For a Latin or Greek Epigram.

Live while you live, the epicure may say,
And snatch the fleeting pleasures of the day:
Live while you live, the sacred preacher cries,
And give to God each moment as it flies:—
Lord, in my view let both united be:
I live in pleasure while I live to Thee.

Into Latin Lyrics.

The sturdy rock, for all his strength,
  By raging seas is rent in twain:
The marble stone is pearst at length,
  With little drops of drizling rain:
The oxe doth yeeld unto the yoke:
The steele obeyeth the hammer stroke.

The stately stagge, that seemes so stout,
  By yalping hounds at bay is set:
The swiftest bird that flies about,
  Is caught at length in fowler's net:
The greatest fish, in deepest brooke,
Is soon deceived by subtil hooke.

Yea man himselfe, unto whose will
  All things are bounden to obey,
For all his wit and worthie skill,
  Doth fade at length, and fall away.
There is nothing but time doeth waste;
The heavens, the earth consume at last.

But vertue sits triumphing still
  Upon the throne of glorious fame:
Though spiteful death man's body kill,
  Yet hurts he not his vertuous name:
By life or death what so betides,
The state of vertue never slides.

Into Latin Prose.

SEVERUS, though now much weakened with age and the gout, yet desirous to leave some memorial of his warlike achievements here, as he had done in other places, and besides to withdraw by this means his two sons from the pleasures of Rome, and his soldiers from idleness, with a mighty power far sooner than could be expected, arrives in Britain. The Northern people, much daunted with the report of so great forces brought over with him, and yet more preparing, send embassadors to treat of peace, and to excuse their former doings. The emperor now loath to return home without some memorable thing done, whereby he might assume to his other titles, the addition of Britannicus, delays his answer, and quickens his preparations; till in the end when all things were in readiness to follow them, they are dismissed without effect.— His principal care was to have many bridges laid over bogs and rotten moors, that his soldiers might have to fight on sure footing. For it seems, through lack of tillage, the northern parts were then, as Ireland is at this day; and the inhabitants in like manner wonted to retire and defend themselves in such watery places half naked. He also, being past Adrian's wall, cut down woods, made way through hills, fastened and filled up unsound and plashy fens. Notwithstanding all this industry used, the enemy kept himself so cunningly within his best advantages and seldom appearing, so opportunely found his times to make irruption upon the Romans, when they were most in straits and difficulties, sometimes training them on with a few cattle turned out, and drawn within ambush cruelly handling them, that many a time enclosed in the midst of sloughs and quagmires, they chose rather themselves to kill such as were faint and could not shift away, than leave them there a prey to the Caledonians. Thus lost Severus, and by sickness in those noisome places, no less than fifty thousand men.

Translate HERODOTUS, *Book* VII. *Chaps.* 76, 77.

Into Greek Prose.

THEY had in their armie above three hundred thousand fighting men, besides a huge multitude of women and children; they wandred over many countries, beating all downe before them; and finally, thinking to have settled themselves in Italy, they divided their company, for the more easie passage thither, and were consumed in three terrible battailes by the Roman consuls. Meere necessity enforced these poore nations to trouble the world, in following such hard adventures. For their country being more fruitfull of men than of sustenance, and shut up on the north side with intolerable cold, which denied issue that way to their overswelling multitudes, they were compelled to discharge upon the south, and by right or wrong to drive others out of possession, as having title to all that they had power to get, because they wanted all, that weaker, but more civill people had. Their sturdy bodies, patient of hunger, cold, and all hardnesse, gave them great advantage over such as were accustomed to a more delicate life, and could not be without a thousand superfluities. Wherefore most commonly they prevailed very farre; their next neighbours giving them free passage, that they might the sooner be ridde of them; others giving them besides passage, victuals and guides to conduct them to more wealthy places; others hiring them to depart with great presents; so as the farther they went on, the more pleasant lands they found, and the more effeminate people.

Into Latin Elegiacs.

Oh what a voice is silent. It was soft
As mountain-echoes, when the winds aloft,
The gentle winds of summer, meet in caves;
Or when in shelter'd places the white waves
Are 'waken'd into music, as the breeze
Dimples, and stems the current: or as trees
Shaking their green locks in the days of June:
Or Delphic girls when to the maiden moon

They sang harmonious pray'rs; or sounds that come
(However near) like a faint distant hum
Out of the grass, from which mysterious birth
We guess the busy secrets of the earth.
Like the low voice of Syrinx, when she ran
Into the forests from Arcadian Pan:
Or sad Œnone's, when she pined away
For Paris, or (and yet 'twas not so gay)
As Helen's whisper when she came to Troy,
Half-shamed to wander with that blooming boy:
Like air-touch'd harps in flowery casements hung;
Like unto lover's ears the wild words sung
In garden-bowers at twilight: like the sound
Of Zephyr when he takes his nightly round,
In May, to see the roses all asleep:
Or like the dim strain which along the deep
The sea-maid utters to the sailor's ear,
Telling of tempests, or of dangers near.
Like Desdemona, who (when fear was strong
Upon her soul) chaunted the willow-song,
Swan-like, before she perish'd; or the tone
Of flutes upon the waters heard alone:
Like words that come upon the memory
Spoken by friends departed; or the sigh
A gentle girl breathes when she tries to hide
The love her eyes betray to all the world beside.

Translate SOPHOCLES, *Antigone, from* v. 100, ἀκτὶς ἀελίου, *to* v. 161, πεμψας, *into English Prose or Latin Lyrics.*

Into Greek Anapæsts or Latin Lyrics.

Now the bright Morning-star, day's harbinger,
Comes dancing from the east, and leads with her
The flow'ry May, who from her green lap throws
The yellow cowslip, and the pale primrose.
  Hail, bounteous May! that dost inspire
  Mirth and youth, and warm desire;
  Woods and groves are of thy dressing,
  Hill and dale doth boast thy blessing.
Thus we salute thee with our early song,
And welcome thee, and wish thee long.

Translate LUCRETIUS, *Book* VI. v. 1143. *Principio,*
    to end.

For Latin Hexameters.

ERE yet the fell Plantagenets had spent
Their ancient rage at Bosworth's purple field;
While, for which tyrant England should receive,
Her legions in incestuous murders mix'd,
And daily horrors; till the fates were drunk
With kindred blood by kindred hands profus'd:
Another plague of more gigantic arm
Arose, a monster never known before,
Rear'd from Cocytus its portentous head.
This rapid fury, not like other pests,
Pursu'd a gradual course, but in a day
Rush'd as a storm o'er half th' astonish'd isle,
And strew'd with sudden carcasses the land.
First through the shoulders, or whatever part

Was seiz'd the first, a fervid vapour sprung;
With rash combustion thence, the quivering spark
Shot to the heart, and kindled all within;
And soon the surface caught the spreading fires;
Through all the yielding pores the melted blood
Gush'd out in smoky sweats; but naught assuag'd
The torrid heat within, nor ought relieved
The stomach's anguish. With incessant toil,
Desperate of ease, impatient of their pain,
They toss'd from side to side. In vain the stream
Ran full and clear, they burnt, aud thirsted still.
The restless arteries with rapid blood
Beat strong and frequent. Thick and pantingly
The breath was fetch'd, and with huge lab'rings heav'd.
At last a heavy pain oppress'd the head,
A wild delirium came; their weeping friends
Were strangers now, and this no home of theirs.
Harass'd with toil on toil, the sinking powers
Lay prostrate and o'erthrown: a ponderous sleep
Wrapt all the senses up: they slept and died.

Into Greek Prose.

✢ GREAT was the heavinesse of the souldiers, being now left destitute of leaders; and no lesse their feare of the evill hanging over their heads, which they knew not well how to avoide. Among the rest Xenophon, whose learning supplied his want of experience, finding the deepe sadnesse of the whole army to be such as hindered them from taking any course of preventing the danger at hand, began to advise the under-officers of Proxenus his companies, whose familiar friend he had been, to bethinke themselves of some meane, whereby their safety might be wrought, and the souldiers encouraged; setting before their eyes whatsoever might serve for to give them hope, and aboue all, perswading them in no wise to yeeld to the mercy of their barbarous enemies. ✢ Hereupon they desired him to take upon him the charge of that regiment; and so together with him, the same night calling up such as were remaining of any account, they made choice of the fittest men to succeed in the places of those who were slain or taken. This being done, and order set downe for disburdening the armie of all superfluous impediments, they easily comforted themselves for the losse of Tissaphernes his assistance, hoping to take victualls by force better cheape than he had been wont to sell them; to which purpose they intended to take up their lodging two or three miles further, among some plentifull villages, and so to proceed, marching towards the heads of those great rivers which lay in their way, and to passe them where they were fordable.

Into Latin or Greek Hexameters.

O MOTHER, hear me yet before I die.
Hear me, O earth—I will not die alone,
Lest their shrill happy laughter come to me
Walking the cold and starless road of death
Uncomforted, leaving my ancient love
With the Greek woman. I will rise and go
Down into Troy, and ere the stars come forth
Talk with the wild Cassandra, for she says
A fire dances before her, and a sound
Rings ever in her ears of armed men.
What this may be I know not, but I know
That, whereso'er I am by night and day,
All earth and air seem only burning fire.

For Latin Alcaics.

Where shall the lover rest,
    Whom the fates sever
From his true maiden's breast,
    Parted for ever?

Where through groves deep and high,
    Sounds the far billow,
Where early violets die,
    Under the willow.

There through the summer-day,
    Cool streams are laving;
There while the tempests sway,
    Scarce are boughs waving;

There thy rest shalt thou take,
    Parted for ever,
Never again to wake—
    Never, O never.

Where shall the traitor rest,
    He the deceiver,
Who could win maiden's breast,
    Ruin, and leave her?

In the lost battle,
    Borne down by the flying,
Where mingles war's rattle
    With groans of the dying.

Her wing shall the eagle flap
    O'er the false-hearted,
His warm blood the wolf shall lap
    Ere life be parted.

Shame and dishonour sit
By his grave ever,
Blessing shall hallow it
Never, O never!

Translate EURIPIDES, *Hippolytus*, v. 611, ὦ Ζεῦ,
to v. 663, ἀεί.

Into Greek Iambics.

OH sacred, shadowy, cold and constant queen,
Abandoner of revels, mute contemplative,
Sweet, solitary, white as chaste, and pure
As wind-fanu'd snow, who to thy female knights
Allow'st no more blood than will make a blush,
Which is their order's robe: I here thy priest
Am humbled 'fore thine altar. Oh! vouchsafe,
With that thy rare green eye, which never yet
Beheld thing maculate, look on thy virgin!
And sacred silver mistress, lend thine ear,
Which ne'er heard scurril term, into whose port
Ne'er enter'd wanton sound, to my petition,
Season'd with holy fear! This is my last
Of vestal office; I'm bride-habited,
But maiden-hearted; a husband I have 'pointed,
But do not know him; out of two I should
Choose one, and pray for his success, but I
Am guiltless of election of mine eyes;
Were I to lose one (they are equal precious)
I could doom neither; that which perish'd should
Go to't unsentenc'd: therefore, most modest queen,
He, of the two pretenders, that best loves me,

And has the truest title in't, let him
Take off my wheaten garland, or else grant
The file and quality I hold I may
Continue in thy band.

Into Latin Elegiacs.

WHEN time shall turn those amber locks to gray,
My verse again shall gild and make them gay,
And trick them up in knotted curls anew,
And to thy autumn give a summer's hue;
That sacred pow'r that in my ink remains
Shall put fresh blood into thy wither'd veins,
And on thy red decay'd, thy whiteness dead,
Shall set a white more white, a red more red:
When thy dim sight thy glass cannot descry,
Nor thy craz'd mirror can discern thine eye;
My verse, to tell th' one what the other was,
Shall represent them both, thine eye and glass:
Where both thy mirror and thine eye shall see,
What once thou saw'st in that, that saw in thee;
And to them both shall tell the simple truth,
What that in pureness was, what thou in youth.

Translate HERODOTUS, *Book* III. *Chap.* 80.

Into Greek Prose.

ARABIA, in the opinion of the naturalist, is the genuine and original country of the *horse*; the climate most propitious, not indeed to the size, but to the spirit and swiftness, of that generous animal. The merit of the Barb, the Spanish, and the English breed, is derived from a mixture of Arabian blood: the Bedoweens preserve, with superstitious care, the honours and the memory of the purest race: the males are sold at a high price, but the females are seldom alienated; and the birth of a noble foal was esteemed among the tribes as a subject of joy and mutual congratulation. These horses are educated in the tents, among the children of the Arabs, with a tender familiarity, which trains them in the habits of gentleness and attachment.—They are accustomed only to walk and to gallop: their sensations are not blunted by the incessant abuse of the spur and the whip; their powers are reserved for the moments of flight and pursuit; but no sooner do they feel the touch of the hand or the stirrup, than they dart away with the swiftness of the wind; and if their friend be dismounted in the rapid career, they instantly stop till he has recovered his seat.

Translate TACITUS, *Annal.* III. 53, 54.

Into Latin Prose.

CHARLES, though engaged in so many wars, was far from neglecting the arts of peace, the happiness of his subjects, or the cultivation of his own mind. Government, manners, religion, and letters, were his constant study. He frequently convened the national assemblies, for regulating affairs both of church and state. In these assemblies he proposed such laws as he considered to be of public benefit, and allowed the same liberty to others: but of this liberty indeed it would have been difficult to deprive the French nobles, who had been accustomed from the foundation of the monarchy to share the legislation with their sovereign. His attention extended to the most distant corner of his empire, and to all ranks of men. Sensible how much mankind in general reverence old customs, and those constitutions under which they have lived from their youth, he permitted the inhabitants of all the countries that he conquered to retain their own laws, making only such alterations as he judged absolutely necessary for the good of the community. He was particularly tender of the common people, and everywhere studied their ease and advantage. This benevolence of mind, which can never be sufficiently admired, was both more necessary and more meritorious in those times, as the commonality were then in a state of almost universal oppression, and scarcely thought entitled to the common sympathies of humanity. The same love of mankind led him to repair and form public roads; to build bridges where necessary; to make rivers navigable for the purposes of commerce; and to project the famous canal which would have opened a communication between the Ocean and the Black Sea, by uniting the Danube and the Rhine. This illustrious project failed in the execution, for want of those machines which art has since constructed; but the greatness of the conception and the honour of having attempted it, were beyond the power of contingences: and posterity has done justice to the memory of Charles, by considering him, on account of this and his other public-spirited plans, as one of those few conquerors who did not merely desolate the earth; as a hero truly worthy of the name, who sought to unite his own glory with the welfare of his species.

Into Latin or Greek Hexameters.

Thus saying, from her husband's hand her hand
Soft she withdrew; and like a wood-nymph light
Oread or Dryad, or of Delia's train,
Betook her to the groves, but Delia's self
In gait surpass'd and goddess-like deport,
Though not as she with bow and quiver arm'd,
But with such gard'ning tools as art, yet rude,
Guiltless of fire, had form'd, or angels brought.
To Pales, or Pomona, thus adorn'd,
Likest she seemed Pomona when she fled
Vertumnus, or to Ceres in her prime,
Yet virgin of Proserpina from Jove.
Her long with ardent look his eye pursu'd
Delighted, but desiring more her stay:
Oft he to her his charge of quick return
Repeated, she to him as oft engaged
To be return'd by noon amid the bow'r,
And all things in best order to invite
Noon-tide repast, or afternoon's repose.

Translate HORACE, *Book* III. *Ode* 29.

Into Latin Lyrics.

No marble statue, nor high
  Aspiring pyramid be raised
To lose its head within the skye!
What claime have I to memory?
  God, be thou onely prais'd.

Thou in a moment canst defeate
The mighty conquests of the proude
And blast the laurels of the great,
Thou canst make brightest glorie set
    O' th' sudden in a cloude.

How can the feeble works of art
Hold out 'gainst the assault of stormes?
Or how can brasse to him impart
Sence of surviving fame, whose heart
    Is now resolved to wormes?

Blinde folly of triumphing pride!
Æternitie, why build'st thou here?
Dost thou not see the highest tide
Its humbled streame in the ocean hide,
    And nere the same appeare?

That tide which did its banckes ore-flow,
As sent abroad by th' angry sea
To levell vastest buildings low
And all our trophes overthrow,
    Ebbes like a theefe away.

And thou, who to preserve thy name,
Leav'st statues in some conquer'd land,
How will posterity scorne fame,
When th' idoll shall receive a maime,
    And loose a foot or hand?

How will thou hate thy warres, when he,
Who onely for his hire did raise
Thy counterfet in stone, with thee
Shall stand competitor, and be
    Perhaps thought worthier praise.

No laurell wreath about my brow!
To thee, my God, all praise, whose law
The conquer'd doth and conqueror bow!
For both dissolve to ayre, if thou
    Thy influence but withdraw.

Translate SOPHOCLES, *Œdipus Coloneus,* v. 632, ἅπανθ'... v. 677, σεσωσμένον.

Into Greek Iambics.

WHAT will the world
Conceive of me? with what unnatural sins
Will they suppose me loaden, when my life
Is sought by her that gave it to the world?
But yet he writes me comfort here: My sister,
He says, is grown in beauty and in grace;
In all the innocent virtues that become
A tender spotless maid: she stains her cheeks
With mourning tears, to purge her mother's ill;
And 'mongst that sacred dew she mingles pray'rs,
Her pure oblations, for my safe return.
If I have lost the duty of a son;
If any pomp or vanity of state
Made me forget my natural offices;
Nay, further, if I have not every night
Expostulated with my wand'ring thoughts,
If ought unto my parent they have err'd,
And call'd 'em back; do you direct her arm
Unto this foul dissembling heart of mine.
But if I have been just to her, send out
Your pow'r to compass me, and hold me safe

From searching treason; I will use no means
But prayer: for rather suffer me to see
From mine own veins issue a deadly flood,
Than wash my danger off with mother's blood.

Into Latin Prose.

From the moment that Belisarius had determined to sustain a siege, his assiduous care provided Rome against the danger of famine, more dreadful than the Gothic arms. An extraordinary supply of corn was imported from Sicily: the harvests of Campania and Tuscany were forcibly swept for the use of the city; and the rights of private property were infringed by the strong plea of the public safety. It might easily be foreseen that the enemy would intercept the aqueducts; and the cessation of the water-mills was the first inconvenience, which was speedily removed by mooring large vessels, and fixing millstones, in the current of the river. The stream was soon embarrassed by the trunks of trees, and polluted with dead bodies; yet so effectual were the precautions of the Roman general, that the waters of the Tiber still continued to give motion to the mills, and drink to the inhabitants: the more distant quarters were supplied from domestic wells; and a besieged city might support without impatience the privation of her public baths. A large portion of Rome, from the Prænestine gate to the church of St. Paul, was never invested by the Goths; their excursions were restrained by the activity of the Moorish troops: the navigation of the Tiber, and the Latin, Appian, and Ostian ways, were left free and unmolested for the introduction of corn and cattle, or the retreat of the inhabitants who sought a refuge in Campania or Sicily. Anxious to relieve himself from an useless and devouring multitude,

Belisarius issued his peremptory orders for the instant departure of the women, the children, and the slaves: required his soldiers to dismiss their male and female attendants, and regulated their allowance, that one moiety should be given in provisions, and the other in money.

Into Greek Prose.

CERTAINLY the miseries of war are never so bitter and many, as when a whole nation, or great part of it, forsaking their own seats, labour to root out the established possessours of another land; making roome for themselves, their wives and children. They that fight for the mastery, are pacified with tribute, or with some other services and acknowledgements; which had they beene yeelded at the first, all had been quiet, and no sword blouded. But in these migrations, the assailants bring so little with them, that they need all which the defendants have, their lands and cattell, their houses and their goods, even to the cradles of the sucking infants. The mercilesse termes of this controversie arme both sides with desperate resolution: seeing the one part must either winne, or perish by famine; the other defend their goods, or lose their lives without redemption. Most of the countries in Europe have felt examples thereof; and the mighty empire of Rome was overthrowne by such invasions.

Into Latin Elegiacs.

OUR bugles sang truce—for the night-cloud had lower'd,
    And the sentinel stars set their watch in the sky;
And thousands had sunk on the ground overpower'd,
    The weary to sleep, and the wounded to die.

When reposing that night on my pallet of straw,
  By the wolf-scaring faggot that guarded the slain,
At the dead of the night a sweet vision I saw,
  And thrice 'ere the morning I dreamt it again.

Methought from the battle-field's dreadful array,
  Far, far I had roam'd on a desolate track:
'Twas Autumn—and sunshine arose on the way
  To the home of my fathers, that welcom'd me back.

I flew to the pleasant fields traversed so oft
  In life's morning march, when my bosom was young;
I heard my own mountain-goats bleating aloft,
  And knew the sweet strain that the corn-reapers sung.

Then pledged we the wine-cup, and fondly I swore
  From my home and my weeping friends never to part;
My little ones kiss'd me a thousand times o'er,
  And my wife sobb'd aloud in her fulness of heart.

Stay, stay with us—rest, thou art weary and worn;
  And fain was their war-broken soldier to stay:
But sorrow return'd with the dawning of morn,
  And the voice in my dreaming ear melted away.

Into Latin Hexameters.

O FOR a lodge in some vast wilderness,
Some boundless contiguity of shade,
Where rumour of oppression and deceit,
Of unsuccessful or successful war,
Might never reach me more. My ear is pain'd,
My soul is sick, with every day's report
Of wrong and outrage, with which earth is fill'd.
There is no flesh in man's obdurate heart,
It does not feel for man; the nat'ral bond

Of brotherhood is sever'd as the flax
That falls asunder at the touch of fire.
He finds his fellow guilty of a skin
Not colour'd like his own; and having pow'r
T' inforce the wrong, for such a worthy cause
Dooms and devotes him as his lawful prey.
Lands intersected by a narrow frith
Abhor each other. Mountains interpos'd
Make enemies of nations, who had else
Like kindred drops been mingled into one.
Thus man devotes his brother, and destroys;
And, worse than all, and most to be deplor'd,
As human nature's broadest, foulest blot,
Chains him, and tasks him, and exacts his sweat
With stripes, that Mercy with a bleeding heart
Weeps, when she sees inflicted on a beast.

Into Latin Lyrics.

WHEN to the sessions of sweet silent thought
I summon up remembrance of things past,
I sigh the lack of many a thing I sought,
And with old woes new wail my dear time's waste:
Then can I drown an eye, unus'd to flow,
For precious friends hid in death's dateless night,
And weep afresh love's long-since cancell'd woe,
And moan the expense of many a vanish'd sight.
Then can I grieve at grievances fore-gone,
And heavily from woe to woe tell o'er
The sad account of fore-bemoaned moan,
Which I new pay as if not paid before.
But if the while I think on thee, dear friend,
All losses are restor'd, and sorrows end.

Into Latin Hexameters.

I SEE a column of slow-rising smoke
O'ertop the lofty wood that skirts the wild.
A vagabond and useless tribe there eat
Their miserable meal. A kettle, slung
Between two poles upon a stick transverse,
Receives the morsel—flesh obscene of dog,
Or vermin, or at best of cock purloin'd
From his accustom'd perch. Hard-faring race!
They pick their fuel out of every hedge,
Which, kindled with dry leaves, just saves unquench'd
The spark of life. The sportive wind blows wide
Their flutt'ring rags, and shews a tawny skin,
The vellum of the pedigree they claim.
Great skill have they in palmistry, and more
To conjure clean away the gold they touch,
Conveying worthless dross into its place;
Loud when they beg, dumb only when they steal.
Strange! that a creature rational, and cast
In human mould, should brutalize by choice
His nature; and, though capable of arts,
By which the world might profit, and himself,
Self-banish'd from society, prefer
Such squalid sloth to honourable toil!
Yet even these, though feigning sickness oft
They swathe the forehead, drag the limping limb,
And vex their flesh with artificial sores,
Can change their whine into a mirthful note,
When safe occasion offers; and with dance,
And music of the bladder and the bag,
Beguile their woes, and make the woods resound.
Such health and gaiety of heart enjoy

The houseless rovers of the sylvan world;
And, breathing wholesome air, and wandering much,
Need other physic none to heal th' effects
Of loathsome diet, penury, and cold.

Into Latin Prose.

They found a province well cultivated, and enjoying plenty, the beauty of the whole earth. They carried their destructive arms into every corner of it; they depeopled it by their devastations, exterminating everything with fire and sword. They did not even spare the vines and fruit-trees, that those, to whom caves and inaccessible mountains had afforded a retreat, might find no nourishment of any kind. Their hostile rage could not be satiated, and there was no place exempted from the effects of it. They tortured their prisoners with the most exquisite cruelty, that they might force from them a discovery of their hidden treasures. The more they discovered, the more they expected, and the more implacable they became. Neither the infirmities of age nor sex, neither the dignity of nobility, nor the sanctity of the sacerdotal office, could mitigate their fury; but the more illustrious their prisoners were the more barbarously they insulted them. The public buildings which resisted the violence of the flames they levelled with the ground. They left many cities without an inhabitant. When they approached any fortified place which their undisciplined army could not reduce, they gathered together a multitude of prisoners, and putting them to the sword, left their bodies unburied, that the stench of the carcases might oblige the garrison to abandon it.

Translate THUCYDIDES, *Book* I. *Chap.* 122.

Into Greek Prose.

THERE is no craving or demand of the human mind more constant and insatiable than that for exercise and employment; and this desire seems the foundation of most of our passions and pursuits. Deprive a man of all business and serious occupation, he runs restless from one amusement to another; and the weight and oppression, which he feels from idleness, is so great that he forgets the ruin which must follow from his immoderate expenses. Give him a more harmless way of employing his mind or body, he is satisfied, and feels no longer that insatiable thirst after pleasure. But if the employment you give him be profitable, especially if the profit be attached to every particular exertion of industry, he has gain so often in his eye, that he acquires, by degrees, a passion for it, and knows no such pleasure as that of seeing the daily increase of his fortune. And this is the reason why trade increases frugality, and why, among merchants, there is the same overplus of misers above prodigals, as, among the possessors of land, there is the contrary.

Translate SOPHOCLES, *Antigone, from* v. 635, οὕτω, *to* v. 719, μανθάνειν.

Into Greek Iambics.

HE that fears death, or tortures, let him leave me!
The stops that we have met with crown our conquest.
Common attempts are fit for common men;

The rare, the rarest spirits. Can we be daunted?
We that have smil'd at sea at certain ruins,
Which men on shore but hazarded would shake at?
We that have liv'd free, in despite of fortune,
Laugh'd at the outstretch'd arm of tyranny,
As still too short to reach us, shall we faint now?
No, my brave mates, I know your fiery temper,
And that you can, and dare, as much as men.
Calamity, that severs worldly friendships,
Could ne'er divide us; you are still the same,
The constant followers of my banish'd fortunes,
The instruments of my revenge, the hands
By which I work, and fashion all my projects.

Into Latin Prose.

✢ IF a man were called to fix upon the period in the history of the world, during which the condition of the human race was most calamitous and afflicted, he would without hesitation name that which elapsed from the death of Theodosius the Great to the establishment of the Lombards in Italy. The contemporary authors, who beheld that scene of desolation, labour, and are at a loss for expressions, to describe the horror of it. *The scourge of God, The destroyer of nations,* are the dreadful epithets by which they distinguish the most noted of the barbarous leaders; and they compare the ruin which they had brought on the world to the havoc occasioned by earthquakes, conflagrations, or deluges, the most formidable and fatal calamities which the imagination of man can conceive. ✢

o But no expressions can convey so perfect an idea of the destructive progress of the barbarians, as that which must strike an attentive observer, when he contemplates the total change which he will discover in the state of Europe, after it began to recover some degree of tranquillity, towards the close of the sixth century. The Saxons were by that time masters of the southern and more fertile provinces of Britain; the Franks of Gaul; the Huns of Pannonia; the Goths of Spain; the Goths and Lombards of Italy, and the adjacent provinces. Very faint vestiges of the Roman policy, jurisprudence, arts, or literature, remained. New forms of government, new laws, new manners, new dresses, new languages, and new names of men and countries, were everywhere introduced.

Into Latin Elegiacs.

† FLATTERED with promise of escape
    From every hurtful blast,
Spring takes, O sprightly May! thy shape—
    Her loveliest and her last.

Less fair is summer riding high
    In fierce solstitial power,
Less fair than when a lenient sky
    Brings on her parting hour.

When earth repays with golden sheaves
    The labours of the plough,
And ripening fruits and forest-leaves
    All brighten on the bough,

What pensive beauty autumn shows,
    Before she hears the sound
Of winter rushing in, to close
    The emblematic round!

Such be our spring, our summer such;
   So may our autumn blend
With hoary winter, and life touch
   Through heaven-born hope, her end. ✚

For Latin Lyrics.

But who the melodies of morn can tell?
The wild brook babbling down the mountain-side;
The lowing herd; the sheepfold's simple bell;
The pipe of early shepherd dim descried
In the low valley; echoing far and wide
The clamorous horn along the cliffs above;
The hollow murmur of the ocean-tide;
The hum of bees, and linnets lay of love,
And the full choir that wakes the universal grove.

The cottage-curs at early pilgrim bark;
Crown'd with her pail the tripping milk-maid sings;
The whistling ploughman stalks a-field; and hark!
Down the rough slope the ponderous waggon rings;
Through rustling corn the hare astonished springs;
Slow tolls the village-clock the drowsy hour;
The partridge bursts away on whirring wings;
Deep mourns the turtle in sequester'd bower,
And shrill lark carols clear from her aërial tour.

Translate Virgil, *Georgic* ii. vv. 298—361.

Into Latin Hexameters.

The stable yields a stercoraceous heap,
Impregnated with quick fermenting salts,
And potent to resist the freezing blast:
For, ere the beech and elm have cast their leaf
Deciduous, when now November dark
Checks vegetation in the torpid plant
Expos'd to his cold breath, the task begins.
Warily therefore, and with prudent heed,
He seeks a favour'd spot; that where he builds
Th' agglomerated pile his frame may front
The sun's meridian disk, and at the back
Enjoy close shelter, wall, or reeds, or hedge
Impervious to the wind. First he bids spread
Dry fern or litter'd hay, that may imbibe
Th' ascending damps; then leisurely impose,
And lightly, shaking it with agile hand
From the full fork, the saturated straw.
What longest binds the closest form secure
The shapely side, that as it rises takes,
By just degrees, an overhanging breadth,
Shelt'ring the base with its projected eaves;
Th' uplifted frame compact at every joint,
And overlaid with clear translucent glass,
He settles next upon the sloping mount,
Whose sharp declivity shoots off secure
From the dash'd pane the deluge as it falls.
He shuts it close, and the first labour ends.

Into Greek Iambics (as in the speech of a messenger).

* * * * * * * *

SHE looked upon him, and was calmed and cheered:
His ghastly colour from his lips had fled:
In his deportment, shape and mien, appeared
Elysian beauty, melancholy grace,
Brought from a pensive though a happy place.

He spake of love, such love as spirits feel
In worlds whose course is equable and pure:
No fears to beat away—no strife to heal—
The past unsighed for, and the future sure:
Spake of heroic arts in graver mood
Revived, with finer harmony pursued:

Of all that is most beauteous, imaged there
In happier beauty—more pellucid streams,
An ampler ether, a diviner air,
And fields invested with purpureal gleams;
Climes which the sun who sheds the brightest day
Earth knows, is all unworthy to survey.

Into Latin Prose.

HE was of person comelier than all his brethren, of pleasing tongue, and graceful behaviour, ready wit and memory; yet through the fondness of his parents towards him, had not been taught to read till the twelfth year of his age; but the great desire of learning which was in him, soon appeared by his conning of Saxon poems day and night, which with great attention he heard by others repeated. He was besides excellent at hunting, and the new art then of hawking, but more exemplary in devotion, having collected into a book certain prayers and psalms, which he carried ever with him in his bosom to use on all occasions. He thirsted after all liberal knowledge, and oft complained that in his youth he had no teachers, in his middle age so little vacancy from wars and the cares of his kingdom; yet leisure he found sometimes, not only to learn much himself, but to communicate thereof what he could to his people, by translating books out of Latin into English, Orosius, Boëthius, Bede's History and others; permitted none unlearned to bear office, either in court or commonwealth.

Into Latin Elegiacs.

I KNOW that all beneath the moon decays,
And what by mortals in this world is brought,
In Time's great periods shall return to nought;
That fairest states have fatal nights and days:
I know how all the Muses' heavenly lays,
With toil of sprite which are so dearly bought,
As idle sounds, of few or none are sought,
And that nought lighter is than airy praise:
I know frail beauty like the purple flower,
To which one morn oft birth and death affords;
That love a jarring is of mind's accords,
Where sense and will envassal reason's power:
Know what I list, this all cannot me move
But that (Oh me!) I both must write and love.

Translate HORACE, *Book* III. *Ode* 3.

Into Latin Lyrics.

✝ Hee who is good is happy. Let the loude
Artillery of heaven breake through a cloud,
And dart its thunder at him, hee'le remaine
Unmov'd, and nobler comfort entertaine
In welcomming th' approach of death, than vice
Ere found in her fictitious paradise.
Time mocks our youth and (while we number past
Delights, and raise our appetite to taste
Ensuing) brings us to unflatter'd age:
Where we are left to satisfie the rage
Of threatning death; pompe, beauty, wealth, and all
Our friendships, shrinking from the funerall.
The thought of this begets that brave disdaine
With which thou view'st the world, and makes those vaine
Treasures of fancy serious fooles so court
And sweat to purchase, thy contempt or sport. ⊥
What should we covet here? Why interpose
A cloud 'twixt us and heaven? kind nature chose
Man's soule th' exchequer where she'd hoord her wealth,
And lodge all her rich secrets; but by th' stealth
Of our own vanity, w' are left so poore,
The creature meerely sensuall knowes more.
The learn'd halcyon by her wisdome finds
A gentle season when the seas and winds
Are silenc't by a calme, and then brings forth
The happy miracle of her rare birth,
Leaving with wonder all our arts possest,
That view the architecture of her nest.
Pride raiseth us 'bove justice—We bestowe
Increase of knowledge on old minds, which grow
By age to dotage: while the sensitive
Part of the world in its first strength doth live.

Into Latin Prose.

The religion of the Arabs, as well as of the Indians, consisted in the worship of the sun, the moon, and the fixed stars—a primitive and specious mode of superstition. The bright luminaries of the sky display the visible image of a Deity: their number and distance convey to a philosophic, or even a vulgar eye, the idea of boundless space: the character of eternity is marked on these solid globes, that seem incapable of corruption or decay: the regularity of their motions may be ascribed to a principle of reason or instinct; and their real or imaginary influence encourages the vain belief, that the earth and its inhabitants are the object of their peculiar care. The science of astronomy was cultivated at Babylon; but the school of the Arabs was a clear firmament and a naked plain. In their nocturnal marches they steered by the guidance of the stars: their names, and order, and daily station, were familiar to the curiosity and devotion of the Bedoween; and he was taught by experience to divide in twenty-eight parts the zodiac of the moon, and to bless the constellations who refreshed with salutary rains the thirst of the desert. The reign of the heavenly orbs could not be extended beyond the visible sphere; and some metaphysical powers were necessary to sustain the transmigration of souls and the resurrection of bodies: a camel was left to perish on the grave, that he might serve his master in another life; and the invocation of departed spirits implies that they were still endowed with consciousness and power.

Into Greek Anapæsts and Iambics.

SHEPHERDS, rise, and shake off sleep!
See the blushing morn doth peep
Through the windows, while the sun
To the mountain tops is run,
Gilding all the vales below
With his rising flames, which grow
Greater by his climbing still.
Up, ye lazy grooms, and fill
Bag and bottle for the field!
Clasp your cloaks fast, lest they yield
To the bitter north-east wind.
 Call the maidens up, and find
Who lay longest, that she may
Go without a friend all day;
Then reward your dogs, and pray
Pan to keep you from decay:
So unfold, and then away.

What! not a shepherd stirring? Sure the grooms
Have found their beds too easy, or the rooms
Fill'd with such new delight, and heat, that they
Have both forgot their hungry sheep, and day.
Knock, that they may remember what a shame
Sloth and neglect lay on a shepherd's name.
It is to little purpose; not a swain
This night hath known his lodging here, or lain
Within these cotes: The woods, or some near town
That is a neighbour to the bord'ring down,
Hath drawn them thither 'bout some lusty sport,
Or spiced wassel-bowl, to which resort
All the young men and maids of many a cote,
Whilst the trim minstrel strikes his merry note,

God pardon sin! shew me the way that leads
To any of their haunts.
    This to the meads,
And that down to the woods.
    Then this for me.
Come, shepherd, let me crave your company.

Translate THUCYDIDES, *Book* III. *Chaps.* 11, 12.

Into Greek Prose.

GREECE was a cluster of little principalities, which soon became republics; and being united both by their near neighbourhood, and by the ties of the same language and interest, they entered into the closest intercourse of commerce and learning. There concurred a happy climate, a soil not unfertile, and a most harmonious and comprehensive language; so that every circumstance among that people seemed to favour the rise of the arts and sciences. Each city produced its several artists and philosophers, who refused to yield the preference to those of the neighbouring republics: their contention and debates sharpened the wits of men: a variety of objects was presented to the judgment, while each challenged the preference to the rest: and the sciences not being dwarfed by the restraint of authority, were enabled to make such considerable shoots, as are, even at this time, the objects of our admiration.

Into Latin Elegiacs.

SWEET to the morning traveller
    The song amid the sky,

Where twinkling in the dewy light
   The sky-lark soars on high.

And cheering to the traveller
   The gales that round him play,
When faint and heavily he drags
   Along his noon-tide way.

And when beneath the unclouded sun
   Full wearily toils he,
The flowing water makes to him
   A soothing melody.

And when the evening light decays,
   And all is calm around,
There is sweet music to his ear
   In the distant sheep-bell's sound.

But oh! of all delightful sounds
   Of evening or of morn,
The sweetest is the voice of love
   That welcomes his return.

For Latin Hexameters.

His eyes he open'd and beheld a field,
Part arable and tilth, whereon were sheaves
New reap'd, the other part sheep-walks and folds:
I' th' midst an altar as the land-mark stood,
Rustic, of grassy sord; thither anon
A sweaty reaper from his tillage brought
Firstfruits, the green ear, and the yellow sheaf,
Uncull'd, as came to hand; a shepherd next
More meek, came with the firstlings of his flock
Choicest and best; then sacrificing laid
The inward and their fat, with incense strew'd,

On the cleft wood, and all due rites perform'd.
His off'ring soon propitious fire from heav'n
Consum'd with nimble glance, and grateful steam;
The other's not, for his was not sincere:
Whereat he inly rag'd, and as they talk'd,
Smote him into the midriff with a stone
That beat out life; he fell, and deadly pale
Groan'd out his life, with gushing blood effused.

Translate LIVY, *Book* III. *Chap.* 36.

Into Latin Prose.

THESE two nations no sooner heard of the departure of the Romans, than they considered the whole island as their own. One party crossed the Forth, in boats made of leather, while another attacked with fury the wall which the Britons had repaired for their defence, but which they abandoned on the first assault, flying like timorous deer, and leaving their country an entire prey to the enemy. The Scots and Picts made a dreadful havoc of the fugitives; and, meeting with no opposition, they laid all the south part of the island waste with fire and sword. Famine followed, with all its horrid train. The miserable Britons, in this frightful extremity, had once more recourse to Rome. They writ to Ætius, then consul the third time, and who governed the empire of the west with an absolute sway, that memorable letter, entitled, *The Groans of the Britons*, and which paints their unhappy condition as strongly as it is possible for words: " We know not," say they, " even which way to flee. Chased by the barbarians to the sea, and forced back by the sea upon the barbarians, we have only left us the choice of two deaths;

either to perish by the sword, or be swallowed up by the waves." What answer they received is uncertain; but it is well known they received no assistance, Rome being then threatened by Attala, the most terrible enemy that ever invaded the empire.

Into Latin Lyrics.

Not love, nor war, nor the tumultuous swell
Of civil conflict, nor the wrecks of change,
Nor duty struggling with afflictions strange,
Not these alone inspire the tuneful shell:
But where untroubled peace and concord dwell
There also is the Muse not loth to range,
Watching the blue smoke of the elmy grange
Sky-ward ascending from the twilight dell.
Meek aspirations please her, lone endeavour,
And sage content, and placid melancholy:
She loves to gaze upon the crystal river
Diaphanous, because it travels slowly;
Soft is the music that would charm for ever:
The flower of sweetest smell is shy and lowly.

Translate HERODOTUS, *Book* VI. *Chap.* 100.

Into Greek Prose.

OTHER nations, the better to observe their solemnities in the due time, and to ascertaine all reckonings and remembrances (which is the principall commodity of time, that is, the measure of endurance), were driven in like manner to make their yeares unequall, by adding sometimes, and sometimes abating one or more dayes, as the error committed in foregoing yeares required. The error grew at first, by not knowing what number of daies made up a compleat yeare. For though, by the continuall course of the sun, causing summer and winter duly to succeed each other, it is plane enough, even to the most savage of all people, when a yeare hath passed over them; yet the necessity of ordinary occurrences, that are to be numbered by a shorter tally, makes this long measure of whole yeares insufficient for the smaller sort of more daily affairs. Therefore men observed the monethly conspicuous revolution of the moone, by which they divided the yeare into twelve parts, subdividing the moneth into twenty-nine dayes and nights, and those again into their quarters and houres. But as the markes of time are sensible and easily discerned: so the exact calculation of it is very intricate, and worketh much perplexity in the understanding. Twelve revolutions of the moone containing lesse time by eleven dayes, or thereabout, than the yearely course of the sunne through the zodiacke. in the space of sixteen years every moneth was found in the quite contrary part of the yeare to that wherein it was placed at the first. This caused them to adde some daies to the yeare, making it to consist of twelve moneths, and as many dayes more, as they thought would make the courses of the sunne and moone to agree. But herein were committed many new errors. For neither did the sunne determine his yearely revolution by any set number of whole days; neither did the moone change always at one houre; but the very minutes and lesser fractions were to be observed by him that would seeke to reduce their motions (which motions also were not still alike) into any certaine rule.

Translate EURIPIDES, *Alcestis*, v. 340, ἔσται τάδ', to v. 380, ἐμοί.

Into Greek Iambics.

HAIL, holy earth, whose cold arms do embrace
The truest man that ever fed his flocks
By the fat plains of fruitful Thessaly!
Thus I salute thy grave; thus do I pay
My early vows and tribute of mine eyes
To thy still-loved ashes;—thus I free
Myself from all ensuing heats and fires
Of love; all sports, delights, and jolly games
That shepherds hold full dear, thus put I off;
Now no more shall these smooth brows be girt
With youthful coronals, and lead the dance;
No more the company of fresh fair maids
And wanton shepherds be to me delightful,
Nor the shrill pleasing sound of merry pipes
Under some shady dell when the cool wind
Plays on the leaves. All be far away,
Since thou art far away, by whose dear side
How often have I sat crown'd with fresh flow'rs
For summer's queen, whilst every shepherd's boy
Puts on his lusty green, with gaudy hook,
And hanging scrip of finest cordevan.
But thou art gone, and these are gone with thee,
And all are dead, but thy dear memory;
That shall out-live thee, and shall ever spring
While there are pipes, or jolly shepherds sing.
And here will I, in honour of thy love,
Dwell by thy grave, forgetting all those joys

That former times made precious to mine eyes;
Only rememb'ring what my youth did gain
In the dark, hidden virtuous use of herbs:
That will I practise, and as freely give
All my endeavours, as I gain'd them free.
Of all green wounds I know the remedies
In men or cattle, be they stung with snakes,
Or charm'd with pow'rful words of wicked art,
Or be they love-sick, or through too much heat
Grown wild or lunatick, their eyes or ears
Thicken'd with misty film of dulling rheum;
These I can cure, such secret virtue lies
In herbs, applied by a virgin's hand.
My meat shall be what these wild woods afford,
Berries and chestnuts, plantanes, on whose cheeks
The sun sits smiling, and the lofty fruit
Pull'd from the fair head of the straight grown pine;
On these I'll feed with free content and rest,
When night shall blind the world, by thy side blest.

Into Latin Prose.

THE character of the people with whom the Romans had to contend was, in all respects, the reverse of theirs. Those northern adventurers, or Barbarians, as they are called, breathed nothing but war; their martial spirit was yet in its vigour; they sought a milder climate, and lands more fertile than their forests and mountains: the sword was their right; and they exercised it without remorse, as the right of nature. Barbarous they surely were, but they were superior to the people they invaded, in virtue as well as in valour. Simple and severe in their manners, they were unacquainted with the word luxury; any thing was sufficient for their extreme frugality: hardened by exercise and toil, their bodies seemed inaccessible to disease or pain: war was their element; they sported with danger, and met death with expressions of joy. Though free and independent, they were firmly attached to their leaders, because they followed them from choice, not from constraint, the most gallant being always dignified with the command. Nor were these their only virtues. They were remarkable for their regard to the sanctity of the marriage-bed; for their generous hospitality; for their detestation of treachery and falsehood: they possessed many maxims of civil wisdom, and wanted only the culture of reason to conduct them to the true principles of social life. ⊥.

For Latin Hexameters.

'Tis said a stranger in the days of old,
Some say a Dorian, some a Sybarite;
(But distant things are ever lost in clouds)
'Tis said a stranger came, and with his plough,
Traced out the site; and Posidonia rose,
Severely great, Neptune the tutelar God;
A Homer's language murmuring in the streets,
And in her haven many a mast from Tyre.
Then came another, an unbidden guest.
He knock'd and enter'd with a train in arms;
And all was changed, her very name and language:
The Tyrian merchant, shipping at his door
Ivory and gold, and silk, and frankincense,
Sail'd as before, but, sailing cried "For Pæstum!"
And now a Virgil, now an Ovid sung
Pæstum's twice-blowing roses; while within,
Parents and children mourn'd—and every year

('Twas on the day of some old festival)
Met to give way to tears, and once again
Talk in the ancient tongue of things gone by.
At length an Arab climb'd the battlements,
Slaying the sleepers in the dead of night;
And from all eyes the glorious vision fled!
Leaving a place lonely and dangerous,
Where whom the robber spares, a deadlier foe
Strikes at unseen—and at a time when joy
Opens the heart, when summer-skies are blue,
And the clear air is soft and delicate;
For then the demon works—then with that air
The thoughtless wretch drinks in a subtle poison
Lulling to sleep; and, when he sleeps, he dies.

Into Latin Elegiacs, or Alcaics.

THE winds are high on Helle's wave,
 As on that night of stormy water
When love, who sent, forgot to save
The young, the beautiful, the brave,
 The lonely hope of Sestos' daughter.
Oh! when alone along the sky
Her turret torch was blazing high,
Though rising gale, and breaking foam,
And shrieking sea-birds warn'd him home;
And clouds aloft and tides below,
With signs and sounds, forbade to go,
He could not see, he would not hear
Or sound or sign foreboding fear;
His eye but saw that light of love,
The only star it hail'd above;

His ear but rang with Hero's song,
" Ye waves divide not lovers long!"—
That tale is old, but love anew
May nerve young hearts to prove as true.
✢ The winds are high, and Helle's tide
    Rolls darkly heaving to the main;
And night's descending shadows hide
    That field with blood bedew'd in vain,
The desert of old Priam's pride;
    The tombs, sole relics of his reign,
All—save immortal dreams that could beguile
The blind old man of Scio's rocky isle. ✢

Translate THUCYDIDES, *Book* IV. *Chaps.* 98, 99.

Into Greek Prose.

CONFEDERATES, we can no longer accuse the Lacedæmonians, they having both decreed the war themselves, and also assembled us to do the same. For it is fit for them who have the command in a common league, as they are honoured of all before the rest, so also, administring their private affairs equally with others, to consider before the rest of the common business. And though as many of us as have already had our turns with the Athenians, need not be taught to beware of them; yet it were good for those that dwell up in the land, and not as we, in places of traffic on the sea-side, to know, that unless they defend those below, they shall with a great deal the more difficulty both carry to the sea the commodities of the seasons, and again more hardly receive the benefits afforded to the inland countries from the sea; and also not to mistake what is now spoken, as if it concerned them not; but to make account, that if they neglect those that dwell by the sea, the calamity will also reach unto themselves;. and that this consultation concerneth them no less than us, and therefore not to be afraid to change their peace for war. For though it be the part of discreet men to be quiet, unless they have wrong, yet it is the part of valiant men when they receive injury, to pass from peace into war, and after success, from war to come again to composition: and neither to swell with the good success of war, nor to suffer injury, through pleasure taken in the ease of peace.

Translate TACITUS, *Annal., Book* VI. 50, 57.

Into Latin Prose.

AFTER bidding adieu to her mourning attendants, with a sad heart, and eyes bathed in tears, Mary left that kingdom, the short but only scene of her life in which fortune smiled upon her. While the French coast continued in sight, she intently gazed upon it, and musing, in a thoughtful posture on that height of fortune whence she had fallen, and presaging, perhaps, the disasters and calamities which embittered the remainder of her days, she sighed often, and cried out, "Farewell, France! farewell, beloved country, which I shall never more behold!" Even when the darkness of the night had hid the land from her view, she would neither retire to the cabin, nor taste food, but commanding a couch to be placed on the deck, she there waited the return of day with the utmost impatience. Fortune soothed her on this occasion; the galley made little way during the night. In the morning, the coast of France was still within sight, and she continned to feed her melancholy with the prospect; and as long as her eyes could distinguish it, to utter the same tender expressions of regret. At last a brisk gale arose, by the favour of which for some days, and afterwards under the cover of a thick fog, Mary escaped the English fleet, which, as she apprehended, lay in wait in order to intercept her; and on the nineteenth of August, after an absence of near thirteen years, landed safely at Leith in her native kingdom.

For Greek Elegiacs, or Latin Alcaics.

WHAT constitutes a state?
    Not high rais'd battlement and labour'd mound,
Thick wall or moated gate:
    Not cities proud, with spires and turrets crown'd:
Not bays and broad-arm'd ports,
    Where, laughing at the storm, rich navies ride:
Not starr'd and spangled courts
    Where low-bred baseness wafts perfume to pride:
No: men, high-minded men,
    With powers as far above dull brutes endu'd,
In forest, brake, or den,
    As beasts excel cold rocks and brambles rude:
Men who their duties know,
    But know their rights; and knowing dare maintain,
Prevent the long-aim'd blow,
    And crush the tyrant, while they rend the chain.

Translate VIRGIL, *Eclogue* VI.

For Latin Hexameters.

FORTH goes the woodman, leaving unconcern'd
The cheerful haunts of man, to wield the axe,
And drive the wedge, in yonder forest drear,
From morn to eve his solitary task.
Shaggy, and lean, and shrewd, with pointed ears
And tail cropp'd short, half lurcher and half cur,
His dog attends him. Close behind his heel
Now creeps he slow; and now, with many a frisk
Wide-scampering, snatches up the drifted snow
With iv'ry teeth, or ploughs it with his snout;
Then shakes his powder'd coat, and barks for joy.
Heedless of all his pranks, the sturdy churl
Moves right toward the mark; nor stops for aught,
But now and then with pressure of his thumb
T' adjust the fragrant charge of a short tube,
That fumes beneath his nose: the trailing cloud
Streams far behind him, scenting all the air.

Translate ÆSCHYLUS, *Prometh.* 658, οὐκ οἶδ᾽ to 704, λόγους.

Into Greek Iambics.

MOST glorious among spirits, thus doth strength
To wisdom, courage, and long-suffering love,
And thee, who art the form they animate,
Minister like a slave.
         Thy gentle words
Are sweeter even than freedom long desired
And long delayed—

Asia, thou light of life,
Shadow of beauty unbeheld: and ye,
Fair sister nymphs, who made long years of pain
Sweet to remember, through your love and care:
Henceforth we will not part. There is a cave,
All overgrown with trailing odorous plants,
Which curtain out the day with leaves and flowers,
And paved with veined emerald, and a fountain
Leaps in the midst with an awakening sound.
From its curved roof the mountain's frozen tears
Like snow, or silver, or long diamond spires,
Hang downward, raining forth a double light:
And there is heard the ever-moving air,
Whispering without form from tree to tree, and birds,
And bees; and all around are mossy seats,
And the rough walls are clothed with long soft grass;
A simple dwelling, which shall be our own;
Where we will sit and talk of time and change,
As the world ebbs and flows, ourselves unchanged.

Into Latin Hexameters.

With Arcita, in stories as men find,
The gret Emetrius the king of Inde,
Upon a stede bay, trapped in stele,
Covered with cloth of gold diapred wele,
Came riding like the god of armes, Mars.
His cote armure was of a cloth of Tars,
Couched with perles, white, and round and grete.
His sadel was of brent gold new ybete;
A mantelet upon his shouldres hanging
Bret-ful of rubies red, as fire sparkling.

His crispe here like ringes was yronne,
And that was yelwe, and glittered as the sonne.
His nose was high, his eyen bright citren,
His lippes round, his colour was sanguin,
A fewe fraknes in his face ysprent,
Betwixen yelwe and blake somdel ymeint,
And as a leon he his looking caste.
Of five and twenty yere his age I caste.
His berd was well begonnen for to spring.
His vois was as a trompe thondering.
Upon his hed he wered of laurer grene
A gerlond fresshe and lusty for to sene.
Upon his hond he bare for his deluit
An egle tame, as any lily whit.
An hundred lordes had he with him there,
All armed save hir hedes, in all hir gere,
Ful richely in alle manere thinges.
For trusteth wel, that erles, dukes, kinges
Were gathered in this noble compaynie
For love, and for enorese of chevalrie.
About this king ther ran on every part
Ful many a tame leon, and leopart.

Into Latin Elegiacs.

LIKE as the waves make towards the pebbled shore,
So do our minutes hasten to their end;
Each changing place with that which goes before,
In sequent toil all forwards do contend.
Nativity once in the main of light,
Crawls to maturity, wherewith being crown'd
Crooked eclipses 'gainst his glory fight,
And time that gave, doth now his gift confound.

Time doth transfix the flourish set on youth,
And delves the parallels in beauty's brow;
Feeds on the rarities of nature's truth,
And nothing stands but for his scythe to mow.
And yet, to times in hope, my verse shall stand,
Praising thy worth, despite his cruel hand.

Translate TACITUS, *Annal.* III. *Chaps.* 26, 27.

For Greek Iambics.

THAT day I oft remember, when from sleep
I first awak'd, and found myself reposed
Under a shade on flow'rs, much wond'ring where
And what I was, whence thither brought, and how:
Not distant far from thence a murmuring sound
Of waters issued from a cave, and spread
Into a liquid plain, then stood unmov'd,
Pure as th' expanse of heav'n; I thither went
With unexperienc'd thought, and laid me down
On the green bank, to look into the clear
Smooth lake, that to me seem'd another sky.
As I bent down to look, just opposite
A shape within the wat'ry gleam appear'd,
Bending to look on me: I started back,
It started back; but pleas'd I soon return'd,
Pleas'd it return'd as soon with answering looks
Of sympathy and love: there I had fix'd
Mine eyes 'till now, and pin'd with vain desire,
Had not a voice thus warn'd me, What thou seest,
What there thou seest, fair creature, is thyself;
With thee it came and goes: but follow me,

And I will bring thee where no shadow stays
Thy coming, and thy soft embraces; he
Whose image thou art, him thou shalt enjoy,
Inseparably thine, to him shalt bear
Multitudes like thyself, and thence be call'd
Mother of human race. What could I do,
But follow straight, invisibly thus led?
'Till I espied thee, fair indeed and tall,
Under a platane; yet, methought, less fair,
Less winning soft, less amiably mild,
Than that smooth wat'ry image.

Translate LIVY, *Book* IV. *Chap.* 9.

Into Latin Prose.

AFTER this first and unsuccessful trial of their enemies, the whole army of the Goths passed the Tiber, and formed the siege of the city, which continued above a year, till their final departure. Whatever fancy may conceive, the severe compass of the geographer defines the circumference of Rome within a line of twelve miles and three hundred and forty-five paces; and that circumference, except in the Vatican, has invariably been the same from the triumph of Aurelian to the peaceful but obscure reign of the modern popes. But in the day of her greatness, the space within her walls was crowded with habitations and inhabitants; and the populous suburbs that stretched along the public roads were darted like so many rays from one common centre. Adversity swept away these extraneous ornaments, and left naked and desolate a considerable part even of the seven hills. Yet Rome, in its present state, could send into the field above thirty thousand males of a military age; and, notwithstanding the want of discipline and exercise, the far greater part, inured to the hardships of poverty, might be capable of bearing arms for the defence of their country and religion. The prudence of Belisarius did not neglect this important resource. His soldiers were relieved by the zeal and diligence of the people, who watched while *they* slept, and laboured while *they* reposed: he accepted the voluntary service of the bravest and most indigent of the Roman youth; and the companies of townsmen sometimes represented, in a vacant post, the presence of the troops which had been drawn away to more essential duties. But his just confidence was placed in the veterans who had fought under his banner in the Persian and African wars; and although that gallant band was reduced to five thousand men, he undertook, with such contemptible numbers, to defend a circle of twelve miles, against an army of one hundred and fifty thousand barbarians.

Into Latin Elegiacs.

THE western waves of ebbing day
Roll'd o'er the glen their level way;
Each purple peak, each flinty spire,
Was bathed in floods of living fire.
But not a setting beam could glow
Within the dark ravines below,
Where twined the path in shadow hid.
Round many a rocky pyramid,
Shooting abruptly from the dell
Its thunder-splinter'd pinnacle;
Round many an insulated mass,
The native bulwarks of the pass,

Huge as the tower which builders vain
Presumptuous piled on Shinar's plain.
The rocky summits, split and rent,
Form'd turret, dome, or battlement,
Or seem'd fantastically set
With cupola or minaret,
Wild crests as pagod ever deck'd,
Or mosque of eastern architect.
Nor were these earth-born castles bare,
Nor lack'd they many a banner fair;
Far from their shiver'd brows display'd
Far o'er the unfathomable glade,
All twinkling with the dew-drops sheen,
The briar-rose fell in streamers green,
And creeping shrubs, of thousand dyes,
Waved in the west-wind's summer sighs.

Into Latin Alcaics.

He who hath never warr'd with misery,
Nor ever tugg'd with fortune and distress,
Hath had n' occasion, nor no field to try
The strength and forces of his worthiness.
Those parts of judgment which felicity
Keeps as conceal'd, affliction must express;
And only men shew their abilities,
And what they are, in their extremities.

The world had never taken so full note
Of what thou art, had'st thou not been undone;
And only thy affliction hath begot
More fame, than thy best fortunes could have done:

For ever by adversity are wrought
The greatest works of admiration;
And all the fair examples of renown
Out of distress and misery are grown.

Mutins the fire, the tortures Regulus,
Did make the miracles of faith and zeal;
Exile renown'd and grac'd Rutilius;
Imprisonment and poison did reveal
The worth of Socrates. Fabritius'
Poverty did grace that commonweal,
More than all Sylla's riches got with strife;
And Cato's death did vie with Cæsar's life.

Not to be unhappy is unhappiness,
And mis'ry not to have known misery;
For the best way unto discretion is
The way that leads us by adversity;
And men are better show'd what is amiss
By the expert finger of calamity,
Than they can be with all that fortune brings,
Who never shews them the true face of things.

He hath a mighty burden to sustain
Whose fortune does succeed a gracious prince;
Or where men's expectations entertain
Hopes of more good, and more beneficence:
But yet he undergoes a greater pain,
A more laborious work, who must commence
The great foundation of a government,
And lay the frame of order and content.

Especially where men's desires do run
A greedy course of eminency, gain,

And private hopes; weighing not what is done
For the republic, so themselves may gain
Their end; and where few care who be undone
So they be made: whilst all do entertain
The present motions that this passage brings
With th' infancy of change, under new kings.

Into Latin Prose.

THE first considerable step towards establishing an equal administration of justice, was the abolishment of the right which individuals claimed of waging war with each other, in their own name, and by their own authority. To repel injuries, and to revenge wrongs, is no less natural to man than to cultivate friendship; and while society remains in its most simple state, the former is considered as a personal right no less unalienable than the latter. Nor do men in this situation deem that they have a title to redress their own wrongs alone; they are touched with the injuries done to those with whom they are connected, or in whose honour they are interested, and are no less prompt to avenge them. The savage, how imperfectly soever he may comprehend the principles of political union, feels warmly the sentiments of social affection, and the obligations arising from the ties of blood; on the appearance of an injury or affront offered to his family or tribe, he kindles into rage, and pursues the authors of it with the keenest resentment. He considers it as cowardly to expect redress from any arm but his own, and as infamous to give up to another the right of determining what reparation he should accept, or with what vengeance he should rest satisfied.

Into Greek Iambics.

Thou cam'st a sharer in a herald's office
Ensuing peace; and cloaked in that disguise,
With money for thy purposes provided,
Thou hast bought treason. This may never pass
Unvisited with penalties extreme;
Else what security is mine that faith
Is not put up to auction in my camp,
'Till each man sell his brother? Who provokes
Treason in others, to a traitor's death
Justly condemns himself. Such is thy lot:
Yet do I rue the judgment I pronounce,
And wish it undeserved; for you have coloured
The darkness of your indirect attempts
With a more lively cheer and gallant bearing
Than most could brighten their best deeds withal.
Sir, I am sorry for you.

Into Latin Prose.

The progress of men in discovering and peopling the various parts of the earth, has been extremely slow. Several ages elapsed before they removed far from those mild and fertile regions in which they were originally placed by their Creator. The occasion of their first general dispersion is known; but we are unacquainted with the course of their migrations, or the time when they took possession of the different countries which they now inhabit. Neither history nor tradition furnishes such information concerning those remote events, as enable us to trace, with any certainty, the operations of the human race in the infancy of society. We may conclude, however, that all the early migrations of mankind were made by land. The ocean, which surrounds the habitable earth, as well as the various arms of the sea which separate one region from another, though destined to facilitate the communication between distant countries, seem, at first view, to be formed to check the progress of man, and to mark the bounds of that portion of the globe to which nature had confined him. It was long, we may believe, before men attempted to pass these formidable barriers, and became so skilful and adventurous as to commit themselves to the mercy of the winds and waves, or to quit their native shores in quest of remote and unknown regions.

Into Latin Lyrics.

Ask me why I send you here,
This firstling of the infant year;
Ask me why I send to you
This primrose all bepearl'd with dew;
I straight will whisper in your ears,
The sweets of love are wash'd with tears.
Ask me why this flow'r doth show
So yellow, green, and sickly too;
Ask me why the stalk is weak,
And bending, yet it doth not break;
I must tell you these discover
What doubts and fears are in a lover.

Translate THUCYDIDES, IV. *Chaps.* 33—35.

Into Greek Prose.

EVERY thing useful to the life of man arises from the ground; but few things arise in that condition which is requisite to render them useful. There must, therefore, beside the peasants and the proprietors of land, be another rank of men, who, receiving from the former the rude materials, work them into their proper form, and retain part for their own use and substance. In the infancy of society, these contracts between the artisans and the peasants, and between one species of artisans and another, are commonly entered into immediately by the persons themselves, who, being neighbours, are easily acquainted with each other's necessities, and can lend their mutual assistance to supply them. But when men's industry increases, and their views enlarge, it is found, that the most remote parts of the state can assist each other as well as the more contiguous, and that this intercourse of good offices may be carried on to the greatest extent and intricacy.

Translate VIRGIL, *Æn.* XI. vv. 763—831.

Into Latin Hexameters.

HIGH on her stately steed the martial maid
Rode foremost of the war! her burnish'd arms
Shone like the brook that o'er its pebbled course
Runs glittering gaily to the noontide sun.
The foaming courser, of her guiding hand
Impatient, smote the earth, and toss'd his mane,
And rear'd aloft with many a froward bound,
Then answered to the rein with such a step,

As, in submission, he were proud to shew
His unsubdued strength. Slow on the air
Waved the white plumes that shadow'd o'er her helm.
Even such, so fair, so terrible in arms
Pelides moved from Scyros, where, conceal'd,
He lay obedient to his mother's fears,
A seemly virgin; thus the youth appear'd
Terribly graceful when upon his neck
Deidameia hung, and with a look
That spake the tumult of her troubled soul,
Fear, anguish, and upbraiding tenderness,
Gazed on the father of her unborn babe.

Into Greek Prose.

THE law of nature in generall, I take to be that disposition, instinct, and formall quality, which God in his eternall providence hath given and imprinted in the nature of every creature, animate and inanimate. And as it is *divinum lumen* in men, inlightning our formall reason; so it is more than sense in beasts; and more than vegetation in plants. For it is not sense alone in beasts, which teacheth them at first sight, and without experience or instruction, to flie from the enemies of their lives; seeing that bulles and horses appeare unto the sense more fearefull and terrible than the least kinde of dogges; and yet the hare and deere feedeth by the one and flieth from the other, yea, though by them never seene before, and that as soone as they fall from their dammes. Neither is it sense which hath taught other beasts to provide for winter, birds to build their nests, high or low, according to the tempestuous or quiet seasons: or the birds of India to make their nests on the smallest twigges which hang over rivers, and not on any other part

of the tree, or else-where: to save their egges and young
ones from the monkies, and other beasts, whose weight such
a twigge will not beare; and which would feare to fall into
the water. The instances in this kinde are exceeding many
which may be given. Neither is it out of the vegitable or
growing nature of plants, that some trees, as the female
of the Palmitto, will not beare any fruit, except the male
grow in sight. But this they do by that law, which the
infinite and unsearchable wisdome of God had in all eternity
provided for them, and for every nature created. In man,
this law is double, corrupt and incorrupt; corrupt, where
the reason of man hath made it selfe subject, and a vassal
to passions, and affections brutall; and incorrupt, where
time and custome hath bred in men a new nature, which
also, as is aforesaid, is a kinde of law.

Translate LUCRETIUS, II. vv. 1—45.

Into Latin Hexameters.

It was a roundell seated on a plaine,
That stood as sentinell unto the maine,
Environ'd round with trees and many an arbour,
Wherein melodious birds did nightly harbour:
And on a bough within the quick'ning spring
Would be a teaching of their young to sing;
Whose pleasing noates the tyred swaine have made
To steale a nappe at noone-tide in the shade.
Nature herselfe did there in triumph ride,
And made that place the ground of all her pride,
Whose various flowres deceiv'd the rasher eye
In taking them for curious tapestrie.

A silver spring forth of a rocke did fall,
That it in a drought did serve to water all.
Upon the edges of a grassie bancke
A tuft of trees grew circling in a rancke,
As if they seem'd their sports to gaze upon,
Or stood as guard against the winde and sunne:
So faire, so fresh, so greene, so sweete a ground,
The piercing eyes of Heaven yet never found.

Into Latin Prose.

I MUST not omit one remarkable action done by him, as Huntingdon reports it, with great scene of circumstance and emphatical expression, to shew the small power of kings in respect of God; which, unless to court-parasites, needed no such laborious demonstration. ✝ He caused his royal seat to be set on the shore, while the tide was coming in; and with all the state that royalty could put into his countenance, said thus to the sea:—Thou, sea, belongest to me, and the land whereon I sit is mine, nor hath any one unpunished resisted my commands: I charge thee come no further upon my land, neither presume to wet the feet of thy sovereign lord. But the sea as before came rolling on, and without reverence both wet and dashed him. Whereat the king quickly rising, wished all about him to behold and consider the weak and frivolous power of a king, and that none indeed deserved the name of a king but he whose eternal laws both heaven, earth, and sea, obey. ✝ A truth so evident of itself, as I said before, that unless to shame his court-flatterers, who would not else be convinced, Canute needed not to have gone wet-shod home. The best is, from that time forth he never would wear a crown, esteeming earthly royalty contemptible and vain.

Into Latin (*Epigrammatic*) Elegiacs.

I stood beneath the castle-wall,
    And mark'd the ivy-bower
That, fragrant in its autumn bloom,
    Wreathed round the mouldering tower.

The plant insinuates its roots
    To rend the ruined wall,
And yet with close and treacherous arms
    Suspends awhile its fall.

I mus'd upon its ancient strength,
    Its hastening dissolution;
And thought upon the ivy friends
    Who prop our Constitution.

Translate Sophocles, *Ajax, from* v. 480, ὦ δέσποτ' ... *to* v. 520, ἀνήρ.

Into Greek Iambics.

'Sweet prince, the name of death was never terrible
To him that knew to live; nor the loud torrent
Of all afflictions, singing as they swim,
A gall of heart, but to a guilty conscience:
Whilst we stand fair, though by a two-edg'd storm
We find untimely falls, like early roses,
Bent to the earth, we bear our native sweetness.'

    'Good sir, go on'—
                  'When we are little children,
And cry, and fret for every toy comes cross us,
How sweetly do we shew when sleep steals on us!

When we grow great, but our affection greater,
And struggle with this stubborn twin, born with us,
And tug and pull, yet still we find a giant;
Had we not then the privilege to sleep
Our everlasting sleep, he'd make us idiots.
The memory and monuments of good men
Are more than lives; and though their tombs want tongues,
Yet have they eyes that daily sweat their losses;
And such a tear from stone no time can value.
To die both young and good, are Nature's curses,
As the world says; ask Truth they're bounteous blessings;
For then we reach at Heav'n in our full virtues,
And fix ourselves new stars, crown'd with our goodness.'

'You've double arm'd me'—

Into Latin Prose.

EARLY in the morning Virginius, in mean attire like a suppliant, led his daughter down to the forum; and some Roman matrons, and a great company of friends, went with him. He appealed to all the people for their aid; "For this," said he, "is not my cause only, but the cause of all." So also spoke Icilius; and the mothers who followed Virginius stood and wept, and their tears moved the people even more than his words. But Appius heeded nothing but his own wicked passion; and before Claudius had done speaking, without suffering Virginius to reply, he hastened to give the sentence. That sentence adjudged the maiden to be considered as a slave till she should be proved to be free-born; and awarded the possession of her in the meanwhile to her master Claudius. Men could scarcely believe that they heard aright, when this monstrous defiance of all law natural and civil was uttered by the very man who had himself enacted the contrary. But when Claudius went to lay hold on the maiden, then the women who stood round her wept aloud, and her friends gathered round her, and kept him off; and Virginius threatened the decemvir that he would not tamely endure so great a wrong. Appius, however, had brought down a band of armed patricians with him; and, strong in their support, he ordered his lictors to make the crowd give way. Then the maiden was left alone before his judgment-seat, till her father, seeing there was no remedy, prayed to Appius that he might speak but one word with her nurse in the maiden's hearing, and might learn whether she were really his own child or no. "If I am indeed not her father, I shall bear her loss the lighter." Leave was given him, and he drew them both aside with him to a spot called afterwards the "new booths;" for tradition kept the place in memory; and there he snatched a knife from a butcher, and said, "This is the only way, my child, to keep thee free," and plunged it in his daughter's heart. Then turning to Appius, "On thee and on thy head," he cried, "be the curse of this blood!" In vain did Appius call out to seize him: he forced his way through the multitude, and still holding the bloody knife in his hand, he made for the gates, and hastened out of the city, and rode to the camp by Tusculum.

Into Latin Lyrics.

WITH how sad steps, O Moon, thou climb'st the skies!
How silently, and with how wan a face!
What! may it be, and even in heavenly place,
That busy Archer his sharp arrows tries?

Sure, if that long with love acquainted eyes
Can judge of love, thou feel'st a lover's case;
I read it in thy looks, thy languish'd grace
To me that feel the like thy state descries.
Then even of fellowship, O Moon, tell me,
Is constant love deem'd there but want of wit?
Are beauties there as proud as here they be?
Do they above love to be lov'd, and yet
Those lovers scorn whom that love doth possess?
Do they call virtue there ungratefulness?

For Latin Hexameters.

FAR in the horrid realms of winter, where
Th' establish'd ocean heaps a monstrous waste
Of shining rocks and mountains to the pole,
There lives a hardy race, whose plainest wants
Relentless earth, their cruel step-mother,
Regards not. On the waste of iron fields,
Untam'd, untractable, no harvests wave;
Pomona hates them, and the clownish god
Who tends the garden. In this frozen world
Such cooling gifts were vain: a fitter meal
Is earn'd with ease: for here the fruitful spawn
Of ocean swarms, and heaps their genial board
With generous fare and luxury profuse.
These are their bread, the only bread they know;
These, and their willing slave, the deer, that crops
The shrubby herbage on their meagre hills.
Girt by the burning zone, not thus the south
Her swarthy sons in either Ind maintains;
Or thirsty Lybia, from whose fervid loins
The lion bursts, and every fiend that roams

Th' affrighted wilderness. The mountain-herd,
Adust and dry, no sweet repast affords:
Nor does the tepid main such kinds produce,
So perfect, so delicious, as the shoals
Of icy Zembla.

Into Latin Prose.

In the use of victory, Constantine neither deserved the praise of clemency, nor incurred the censure of immoderate rigour. He inflicted the same treatment to which a defeat would have exposed his own person and family— put to death the two sons of the tyrant, and carefully extirpated his whole race. The most distinguished adherents of Maxentius must have expected to share his fate, as they had shared his prosperity and his crimes; but when the Roman people loudly demanded a greater number of victims, the conqueror resisted, with firmness and humanity, those servile clamours which were dictated by flattery as well as by resentment. Informers were punished and discouraged; the innocent, who had suffered under the late tyranny, were recalled from exile, and restored to their estates. A general act of oblivion quieted the minds, and settled the property of the people, both in Italy and in Africa. The first time that Constantine honoured the senate with his presence, he recapitulated his own services and exploits in a modest oration, assured that illustrious order of his sincere regard, and promised to re-establish its ancient dignity and privileges. The grateful senate repaid these unmeaning professions by the empty titles of honour, which it was yet in their power to bestow; and without presuming to ratify the authority of Constantine, they passed a decree to assign him the first rank among the three *Augusti* who governed the Roman world. Games and festivals were instituted to preserve the fame of his victory; and several edifices raised at the expense of Maxentius, were dedicated to the honour of his successful rival. ✢ The triumphal arch of Constantine still remains a melancholy proof of the decline of the arts, and a singular testimony of the meanest vanity. As it was not possible to find in the capital of the empire a sculptor who was capable of adorning that public monument, the arch of Trajan, without any respect either for his memory or for the rules of propriety, was stripped of its most elegant figures. The difference of times and persons, of actions and characters, was totally disregarded. The Parthian captives appear prostrate at the feet of a prince who never carried his arms beyond the Euphrates; and curious antiquarians can still discover the head of Trajan on the trophies of Constantine. The new ornaments which it was necessary to introduce between the vacancies of ancient sculpture, are executed in the rudest and most unskilful manner.

Into Latin Elegiacs.

FORSAKE me not so soone. Castara, stay,
And as I breake the prison of my clay
Ile fill the canvas with m'expiring breath.
And with thee saile o'er the vast maine of death.
Some cherubin thus as we passe shall play:
"Goe, happy twins of love!" the courteous sea
Shall smooth her wrinkled brow: the winds shall sleep,
Or onely whisper musicke to the deepe.
Every ungentle rocke shall melt away,
The syrens sing to please, not to betray.

Th' indulgent skie shall smile; each starry quire
Contend which shall afford the brighter fire.
While Love the pilot steers his course so even,
Neere to cast-anchor till we reach at Heaven.

Translate THUCYDIDES, *Book* III. *Chap.* 38.

Into Greek Prose.

THAT which he notes especially to be the chief perverting of all good in the land, and so continued in his days, was the hatred of truth, and all such as durst appear to vindicate and maintain it against them, as against the only disturbers, all the malice of the land was bent. Lies and falsities, and such as could best invent them, were only in request. Evil was embraced for good, wickedness honoured and esteemed as virtue. And this quality their valour had against a foreign enemy, to be ever backward and heartless; to civil broils eager and prompt. In matters of government and the search of truth, weak and shallow, in falsehood and wicked deeds pregnant and industrious. Pleasing to God, or not pleasing, with them weighed alike, and the worse most an end was the weightier. All things were done contrary to public welfare and safety— nor only by secular men, for the clergy also, whose example should have guided others, were as vicious and corrupt. Many of them besotted with continual drunkenness, or swoln with pride and wilfulness, full of contention, full of envy, indiscreet, incompetent judges to determine what in the practice of life is good or evil, what lawful or unlawful.

Translate HORACE, *Book* III. *Ode* 27.

Into Latin Sapphics.

It is not that my lot is low,
That bids the silent tear to flow;
It is not grief that bids me moan,
It is that I am all alone.

In woods and glens I love to roam,
When the tired hedger hies him home;
Or by the woodland pool to rest,
When pale the star looks on its breast.

Yet when the silent evening sighs
With hallow'd airs and symphonies,
My spirit takes another tone,
And sighs that it is all alone.

The autumn leaf is sear and dead,
It floats upon the water's bed;
I would not be a leaf, to die
Without recording sorrow's sigh!

The woods and winds, with sudden wail,
Tell all the same unvaried tale;
I've none to smile when I am free,
And when I sigh, to sigh with me.

Yet in my dreams a form I view,
That thinks on me, and loves me too;
I start, and when the vision's flown,
I weep that I am all alone.

Translate TACITUS, *Annal.* VI. 50, 51.

Into Latin Prose.

THE Britons thus, as we heard, being left without protection from the empire, and the land in a manner emptied of all her youth, consumed in wars abroad, or not caring to return home, themselves through long subjection servile in mind, slothful of body, and with the use of arms unacquainted, sustained but ill for many years the violence of those barbarous invaders who now daily grew upon them. For although at first greedy of change, and to be thought the leading nation to freedom from the empire, they seemed a while to bestir them with a shew of diligence in their new affairs, some secretly aspiring to rule, others adoring the name of liberty, yet so soon as they felt by proof the weight of what it was to govern well themselves, and what was wanting within them, not stomach or the love of license, but the wisdom, the virtue, the labour, to use and maintain true liberty, they soon remitted their heat, and shrunk more wretchedly under the burden of their own liberty, than before under a foreign yoke.

Translate HERODOTUS, II. 120.

Into Greek Prose.

HE that suspecteth his owne worth or other men's opinions, thinking the lesse regard is had of his person than he beleeveth to be due to his place, will commonly spend all the force of his authoritie in purchasing the name of a severe man. For the affected sowrenesse of a vaine fellow, doth many times resemble the gravity of one that is wise; and the feare wherein they live, which are subject unto oppression, carryes a shew of reverence to him that does the wrong; at least it serves to dazle the eyes of underlings, keeping them from prying into the weaknesse of such as have jurisdiction over them. Thus the time, wherein, by well using it, men might attaine to be such as they ought, they do usually mispend, in seeking to appeare such as they are not. This is a vain and deceivable course; procuring, instead of the respect that was hoped for, more indignation than was feared. Which is a thing of dangerous consequence; especially when an unable spirit, being over-perted with so high authority, is too passionate in the execution of such an office, as cannot be checked but by violence.

Into Latin Elegiacs.

Cupid and my Campaspe play'd
At cardes for kisses; Cupid pay'd;
He stakes his quiver, bow and arrows,
His mother's doves, and teame of sparrows;
Loses them too; then down he throws
The coral of his lippe, the rose
Growing on 's cheek, (but none knows how),
With these, the crystal of his browe,
And then the dimple of his chinne;
All these did my Campaspe winne.
At last he set her both his eyes,
She won, and Cupid blind did rise.
    O Love! has she done this to thee?
    What shall, alas! become of me?

Translate Euripides, *Orestes*, vv. 1—70.

Into Greek Iambics.

DIRE rebel though he was,
Yet with a noble nature and great gifts
Was he endowed: courage, discretion, wit,
An equal temper, and an ample soul,
Rock-bound and fortified against assaults
Of transitory passion, but below
Built on a surging subterranean fire
That stirred and lifted him to high attempts.
So prompt and capable, and yet so calm,
He nothing lacked in sovereignty but the right;
Nothing in soldiership except good fortune.
Wherefore with honour lay him in the grave,
And thereby shall increase of honour come
Unto their arms who vanquished one so wise,
So valiant, so renowned.

Translate LIVY, *Book* IV. *Chaps.* 2—5.

Into Latin Prose.

WHAT cruel tyrants were the Romans over the world during the time of their commonwealth! It is true they had laws to prevent oppression in their provincial magistrates; but Cicero informs us, that the Romans could not better consult the interest of the provinces than by repealing these very laws. For in that case, says he, our magistrates, having entire impunity, would plunder no more than would satisfy their own rapaciousness; whereas, at present, they must also satisfy that of their judges, and of all the great men of Rome, of whose protection they stand in need. Who can read of the cruelties and oppressions of Verres without horror and astonishment? And who is not touched with indignation to hear, that, after Cicero had exhausted on that abandoned criminal all the thunders of his eloquence, and had prevailed so far as to get him condemned to the utmost extent of the laws; yet that cruel tyrant lived peaceably to old age, in opulence and ease, and, thirty years afterwards, was put into the proscription by Mark Anthony, on account of his exorbitant wealth, where he fell with Cicero himself, and all the most virtuous men of Rome? After the dissolution of the commonwealth, the Roman yoke became easier upon the provinces, as Tacitus informs us; and it may be observed, that many of the worst emperors, Domitian for instance, were careful to prevent all oppression on the provinces. In Tiberius' time, Gaul was esteemed richer than Italy itself. Nor do I find during the whole time of the Roman monarchy, that the empire became less rich or populous in any of its provinces, though indeed its valour and military discipline were always upon the decline.

Translate VIRGIL, *Æn.* VIII. 608—661.

Into Latin Hexameters.

IF rich designs of sumptuous art may please,
   Or nature's loftier views, august and old,
   Stranger, behold this spreading scene; behold
This amphitheatre of aged trees,
That solemn wave above thee, and around
   Darken the tow'ring hills! Dost thou complain
   That thou should'st cope with penury or pain,

Or sigh to think what pleasure might be found
Amid such wide possessions? Pause awhile—
Imagine thou dost see the sick man smile,
See the pale exiles that in yonder dome,
Safe from the wasteful storm, have found a home;
And thank the Giver of all good, that lent
To the humane, retired beneficent,
The pow'r to bless:—nor lift thy heart elate,
If such domains be thine; but emulate
The fair example, and those deeds, that rise
Like holy incense wafted to the skies—
Those deeds that shall sustain the conscious soul,
When all this empty world is perish'd, like a scroll!

Into Latin Elegiacs.

Gone from her cheek is the summer-bloom,
And her lip has lost all its faint perfume;
And the gloss has dropp'd from her golden hair,
And her cheek is pale, but no longer fair.

And the spirit that sate on her soft blue eye,
Is struck with cold mortality;
And the smile that play'd round her lip has fled,
And every charm has now left the dead.

Like slaves they obey'd her in height of power,
But left her all in her wintry hour;
And the crowds that swore for her love to die,
Shrunk from the tone of her last faint sigh.
———And this is man's fidelity!

'Tis woman alone, with a purer heart,
Can see all these idols of life depart,
And love the more, and smile and bless
Man in his uttermost wretchedness.

Translate THUCYDIDES, IV. 98, 99.

Into Greek Prose.

THIS was the last worke of the incomparable vertue of Epaminondas, who being in the head of that warlike troupe of men, which broke the Lacedæmonian esquadron, and forced it to give back in disaray, was furiously charged on the sudden, by a desperate companie of the Spartans, who all at once threw their darts at him alone; whereby receiving many wounds, he neverthelesse with a singular courage maintained the fight, using against the enemies many of their darts, which he drew out of his owne bodie; till at length, by a Spartan, called Anticrates, he received so violent a stroke with a dart, that the wood of it brake, leaving the yron and a peece of the trunchion in his breast. Hereupon he sunk down, and was soon conveyed out of the fight by his friends; having by his fall somewhat animated the Spartans (who fain would have got his bodie), but much more inflamed with revengefull indignation the Thebans, who raging at this heavy mischance, did with great slaughter compell their disordered enemies to leave the field; though long they followed not the chase, being wearied more with the sadnesse of this disaster, than with all the travell of the day. Epaminondas being brought into his tent, was told by the physicians, that when the head of the dart should be drawn out of his bodie, he must needs dye. Hearing this, he called for his shield, which to have lost was held a great dishonour: it was brought unto him. He bad them tell him which part had the victorie; answer was made, that the Bœotians had won the field. Then said he, "It is faire time for me to dye;"—and withall sent for Iolidas and

Diophantes, two principal men of war, that were both slain; which being told him, he advised the Thebans to make peace, whilest with advantage they might, for that they had none left that was able to discharge the office of a general. Therewithall he willed, that the head of the weapon should be drawn out of his body, comforting his friends that lamented his death, and want of issue, by telling them that the victories of Leuctra and Mantinæa were two faire daughters, in whom his memorie should live.

For Latin Elegiacs.

Such were the notes that from the pirate's isle
Around the kindling watch-fire rang the while;
Such were the sounds that thrill'd the rocks along,
And unto ears as rugged seem'd a song!
In scatter'd groups upon the golden sand,
They game—carouse—converse—or whet the brand;
Select the arms—to each his blade assign,
And careless eye the blood that dims its shine;
Repair the boat, replace the helm or oar,
While others straggling muse along the shore;
For the wild bird the busy springes set,
Or spread beneath the sun the dripping net;
Gaze where some distant sail a speck supplies,
With all the thirsting eye of enterprize;
Tell o'er the tales of many a night of toil,
And marvel where they next shall seize a spoil:
No matter where—their chief's allotment this;
Theirs, to believe no prey nor plan amiss.

Translate Sophocles, *Œdipus Coloneus, from* v. 1583, ὡς μὲν, *to* v. 1662, φρονεῖν.

Into Greek Iambics.

'Tis not the white or red
Inhabits in your cheek that thus can wed
My mind to adoration; nor your eye,
Though it be full and fair, your forehead high,
And smooth as Pelops' shoulder; not the smile
Lies watching in those dimples to beguile
The easy soul; your hands and fingers long,
With veins enamell'd richly; nor your tongue,
Though it spoke sweeter than Arion's harp;
Your hair woven into many a curious warp,
Able in endless error to enfold
The wand'ring soul; not the true perfect mould
Of all your body, which as pure doth shew
In maiden whiteness as the Alpsien snow;
All these, were but your constancy away,
Would please me less than a black stormy day
The wretched seaman toiling through the deep.
But while this honour'd strictness you dare keep,
Though all the plagues that e'er begotten were
In the great womb of air, were settled here,
In opposition, I would, like the tree,
Shake off those drops of weakness, and be free
Ev'n in the arm of danger.

Into Latin Hexameters.

As when a dainty fount and christall spring,
Got newly from the earth's imprisoning,
And ready prest some channell cleere to win,
If round his rise by rockes immured in,
And from the thirsty earth would be withheld,
Till to the cesterne toppe the waves have swell'd:
But that a carefull hinde the well hath found,
As he walkes sadly through his parched ground;
Whose patience suff'ring not his land to stay
Until the water o'er the cesterne play,
He gets a picke-axe, and with blowes so stout,
Digs on the rocke, that all the groves about
Resound his stroke, and still the rocke doth charge,
Till he hath made a hole both long and large,
Whereby the waters from their prison run,
To close earth's gaping wounds made by the sun.

Translate TACITUS, *Annal.* II. 71, 72.

Into Latin Prose.

I SHALL also be bold to affirm, that among the ancients there was not much delicacy of breeding, or that polite deference and respect, which civility obliges us either to express or counterfeit towards the persons with whom we converse. Cicero was certainly one of the finest gentlemen of his age; yet I must confess I have frequently been shocked with the poor figure under which he represents his friend Atticus, in those dialogues where he himself is introduced as a speaker. That learned and virtuous Roman, whose dignity, though he was only a private gentleman, was inferior to that of no one in Rome, is there shewn in rather a more pitiful light than Philalethes's friend in our modern dialogues. He is a humble admirer of the orator, pays him frequent compliments, and receives his instructions with all the deference a scholar owes to his master. Even Cato is treated in somewhat a cavalier manner in the dialogues *de finibus*.

One of the most particular details of a real dialogue which we meet with in antiquity is related by Polybius; when Philip, king of Macedon, a prince of wit and parts, met with Titus Flamininus, one of the politest of the Romans, as we learn from Plutarch, accompanied with ambassadors from almost all the Greek cities. The Ætolian ambassador very abruptly tells the king that he talked like a fool or a madman, (λήρειν). *That's evident*, says his majesty, *even to a blind man;* which was a raillery on the blindness of his excellency. Yet all this past not the usual bounds: for the conference was not disturbed: and Flamininus was very well diverted with these strokes of humour. At the end, when Philip craved a little time to consult with his friends, of whom he had none present, the Roman general, being desirous also to shew his wit, as the historian says, tells him *that perhaps the reason why he had none of his friends with him, was because he had murdered them all;* which was actually the case. This unprovoked piece of rusticity is not condemned by the historian; caused no farther resentment in Philip, than to excite a sardonian smile, or what we call a grin; and hindered him not from renewing the conference next day.

Into Latin Elegiacs.

† TO THE SNOWDROP.

BENEATH the chilling airs, when I behold
   Thee, lovely flow'r, recline thy languid head:
When I behold thee drooping, pale, and cold,
   And sorrowing for thy vernal sisters dead;
Methinks I mark the orphan child of woe,
   Exposed to hardship from his earliest birth,
Bending beneath the wintry storms that blow,
   His only portion a rude spot of earth;
Yet sure like thine, meek flow'r, his spring draws near,
And Heav'n's sweet sunshine shall inhale each tear. ┼

Translate THUCYDIDES, *Book* I. *Ch.* 138.

For Greek (Thucydidean) *Prose.*

So died Epaminondas, the worthiest man that ever was bred in that nation of Greece, and hardly to be matched in any age or countrie; for he equalled all others in the severall vertues, which in each of them were singular. His justice and sinceritie, his temperance, wisedome, and high magnanimitic, were no way inferior to his militarie vertue; in every part whereof he so excelled, that he could not properly be called a warie, a valiant, a politique, a bountifull, or an industrious, and a provident captaine. Neither was his private conversation unanswerable to those high parts which gave him praise abroad. For he was grave, and yet very affable and courteous; resolute in publique businesse, but in his owne particular easie, and of much mildenesse: a lover of his people, bearing with men's infirmities; wittie and pleasant in speech, far from insolence, master of his own affections, and furnished with all qualities that might win and keepe love. To these graces were added great abilitie of bodie, much eloquence, and very deep knowledge in all parts of philosophie and learning, wherewith his minde being enlightened, rested not in the sweetnesse of contemplation, but brake forth into such effects as gave unto Thebes, which had ever-more bin an underling, a dreadfull reputation among all people adjoyning, and the highest command in Greece.

Into Latin Elegiacs.

HE who hath bent him o'er the dead,
'Ere the first day of death is fled;
The first dark day of nothingness,
The last of danger and distress;
(Before decay's effacing fingers
Have swept the lines where beauty lingers)
And mark'd the mild angelic air—
The rapture of repose that's there—
The fix'd yet tender traits that streak
The languor of the placid cheek,
And—but for that sad shrowded eye,
That fires not—wins not, weeps not—now,
And but for that chill changeless brow,
Where cold obstruction's apathy
Appals the gazing mourner's heart,
As if to him it could impart
The doom he dreads, yet dwells upon—
Yes, but for these, and these alone,
Some moments, aye, one treach'rous hour,
He still might doubt the tyrant's power,

So fair, so calm, so softly seal'd,
The first, last look, by death reveal'd.
Such is the aspect of this shore—
'Tis Greece—but living Greece no more!

Into Latin Prose.

ONCE Titus and Aruns were supping with their brother Sextus, and their cousin Tarquinius of Collatia was supping with them. And they disputed about their wives, whose wife of them all was the worthiest lady. Then said Tarquinius of Collatia, "Let us go and see with our own eyes what our wives are doing, so shall we know which is the worthiest." Upon this they all mounted their horses, and rode first to Rome; and there they found the wives of Titus, and of Aruns and of Sextus, feasting and making merry. Then they rode on to Collatia, and it was late in the night, but they found Lucretia, the wife of Tarquinius of Collatia, neither feasting, nor yet sleeping, but she was sitting with all her handmaids around her, and all were working at the loom. So when they saw this, they all said, "Lucretia is the worthiest lady." And she entertained her husband and his kinsmen, and after that they rode back to the camp before Ardea.

Translate EURIPIDES, *Medea, from* v. 1015, δράσω τάδ', *to* 1076, βροτοῖς.

Into Greek Iambics.

CARE-CHARMER Sleep, son of the sable Night,
Brother to death, in silent darkness born,

Relieve my languish, and restore the light,
With dark forgetting of my care's return;
And let the day be time enough to mourn
The shipwreck of my ill-adventur'd youth;
Let waking eyes suffice to wail their scorn,
Without the torment of the night's untruth.
Cease, dreams, the images of day-desires,
To model forth the passions of the morrow;
Never let rising sun approve you liars,
To add more grief to aggravate my sorrow.
Still let me sleep, embracing clouds in vain,
And never wake to feel the day's disdain.

Into Latin Prose.

✷. THE life of Belisarius was graciously spared, but his fortunes were sequestered; and from December to July he was guarded as a prisoner in his own palace. At length his innocence was acknowledged: his freedom and honours were restored; and death, which might be hastened by resentment and grief, removed him from the world about eight months after his deliverance. The name of Belisarius can never die: but instead of the funeral, the monuments, the statues, so justly due to his memory, I only read that his treasures, the spoils of the Goths and Vandals, were immediately confiscated by the emperor. Some decent portion was reserved, however, for the use of his widow; and as Antonina had much to repent, she devoted the last remains of her life and fortune to the foundation of a convent. Such is the simple and genuine narrative of the fall of Belisarius, and the ingratitude of Justinian. That he was deprived of his eyes, and reduced by envy to beg his bread: " Give a penny to Belisarius the general!" is a fiction of later times, which has obtained credit, or rather favour, as a strange example of the vicissitudes of fortune.

For Latin Elegiacs.

FOUNTAIN, that sparklest through the shady place,
　Making a soft sad murmur o'er the stones
That strew thy lucid way! Oh, if some guest
　Should haply wander near, with slow disease
Smitten, may thy cold springs the rose of health
　Bring back, and the quick lustre to his eye!
The ancient oaks that on thy margin wave,
　The song of birds, and through the rocky cave
The clear stream gushing, their according sounds
　Should mingle, and like some strange music, steal
Sadly, yet soothing, o'er his aching breast.
And thou pale exile from thy native shores,
　Here drink, (O could'st thou! as of Lethe's stream)
Nor friends, nor bleeding country, nor the views
　Of hills or streams beloved, nor vesper's bell,
Heard in the twilight vale, remember more!

Translate THUCYDIDES, *Book* II. *Chap.* 77.

Into Greek Prose.

THE life of the emperor Alexius has been delineated by a favorite daughter, who was inspired by a tender regard for his person, and a laudable zeal to perpetuate his virtues. Conscious of the just suspicion of her readers, the princess Anna Comnena repeatedly protests, that, besides her personal knowledge, she had searched the discourse and writings of the most respectable veterans: that after an interval of thirty years, forgotten by, and forgetful of, the world, her mournful solitude was inaccessible to hope and fear; and that truth, the naked perfect truth, was more dear and sacred than the memory of her parent: yet, instead of the simplicity of style and narrative which wins our belief, an elaborate affectation of rhetoric and science betrays in every page the vanity of a female author. The genuine character of Alexius is lost in a vague constellation of virtues; and the perpetual strain of panegyric and apology awakens our jealousy, to question the veracity of the historian, and the merit of the hero.

Translate HORACE, *Epod.* 16.

Into Latin Lyrics.

THE gift to king Amphion
That walled a city with its melody
Was for belief no dream; thy skill, Arion!
Could humanise the creatures of the sea,
Where men were monsters. A last grace he craves,
Leave for one chant;—the dulcet sound
Steals from the deck o'er willing waves,
And listening dolphins gather round.
Self-cast, as with a desperate course,
'Mid that strange audience, he bestrides
A proud one, docile as a managed horse;
And singing, while the accordant hand
Sweeps his harp, the master rides;
So shall he touch at length a friendly strand,

And he with his preserver, shine star-bright
In memory, through silent night.

The pipe of Pan, to shepherds
Couched in the shadow of Menalian pines
Was passing sweet; the eye-balls of the leopards,
That in high triumph drew the lord of vines,
How did they sparkle to the cymbal's clang!
While fauns and satyrs beat the ground
In cadence—and Silenus swang
This way and that, with wild-flowers crown'd.

Into Greek Prose.

HAPPILY for the repose of mankind, the moderate system recommended by the wisdom of Augustus was adopted by the fears and vices of his immediate successors. Engaged in the pursuit of pleasure, or in the exercise of tyranny, the first Cæsars seldom shewed themselves to the armies, or to the provinces; nor were they disposed to suffer, that those triumphs which their indolence neglected, should be usurped by the conduct and valour of their lieutenants. The military fame of a subject was considered as an insolent invasion of the imperial prerogative; and it became the duty, as well as interest, of every Roman general, to guard the frontiers intrusted to his care, without aspiring to conquests, which might have proved no less fatal to himself than to the vanquished barbarians.

Translate LUCRETIUS, *Book* v. *from* v. 282, *Largus item*.... *to* v. 330, *florent.*

Into Latin Hexameters.

YET I had rather, if I were to choose,
Thy service in some graver subject use,
Such as may make thee search thy coffers round,
Before thou clothe my fancy in fit sound:
Such where the deep transported mind may soar
Above the wheeling poles, and at heav'n's door
Look in, and see each blissful Deity
How he before the thunderous throne doth lie,
List'ning to what unshorn Apollo sings
To th' touch of golden wires, while Hebe brings
Immortal nectar to her kingly sire;
Then passing through the spheres of watchful fire,
And misty regions of wide air next under,
And hills of snow, and lofts of piled thunder,
May tell at length how green-ey'd Neptune raves,
In heav'n's defiance mustering all his waves;
Then sing of secret things that came to pass
When beldam nature in her cradle was;
And last of kings and queens and heroes old,
Such as the wise Demodocus once told,
In solemn songs at king Alcinous' feast,
While sad Ulysses' soul, and all the rest
Are held with his melodious harmony,
In willing chains and sweet captivity.

Into Greek Anapæsts: or Latin Lyrics.

  NYMPHS and shepherds, dance no more
    By sandy Ladon's lilied banks:
  On old Lycæus or Cyllene hoar
    Trip no more in twilight ranks;

Though Erymanth your loss deplore,
  A better soil shall give you thanks.
From the stony Mænalus
Bring your flocks, and live with us;
There ye shall have greater grace,
To serve the Lady of this place.
Though Syrinx your Pan's mistress were,
Yet Syrinx well might wait on her.
  Such a rural queen
  All Arcadia hath not seen.

Into Latin Elegiacs.

ONCE did she hold the gorgeous East in fee;
And was the safeguard of the West: the worth
Of Venice did not fall below her birth—
Venice, the eldest child of Liberty.
She was a maiden city, bright and free;
No guile seduced, no force could violate;
And, when she took unto herself a mate,
She must espouse the everlasting sea.
And what if she had seen those glories fade,
Those titles vanish, and that strength decay;
Yet shall some tribute of regret be paid
When her long life hath reached its final day:
Men are we, and must grieve when even the shade
Of that which once was great is passed away.

Into Latin Prose.

AFTER this King Leir, more and more drooping with years, became an easy prey to his daughters, and their husbands; who now by daily encroachment had seiz'd the whole kingdom into their hands: and the old king is put to sojourn with his eldest daughter, attended only by threescore knights. But they in a short while grudged at, as too numerous and disorderly for continual guests, are reduced to thirty. Not brooking that affront, the old king betakes him to his second daughter; but there also discord soon arising between the servants of differing masters in one family, five only are suffered to attend him. Then back again he returns to the other; hoping that she his eldest could not but have more pity on his grey hairs; but she now refuses to admit him, unless he be content with one only of his followers. At last the remembrance of his youngest, Cordeilla, comes to his thoughts; and now, acknowledging how true her words had been, though with little hope from whom he had so injured, be it but to pay the last recompense she can have from him, his confession of her wise forewarning, that so perhaps his misery (the proof and experiment of her wisdom) might something soften her, he takes his journey into France.

Translate SOPHOCLES, *Ajax, from* v. 480, ὦ δεσπότ',
to v. 520, ἀνήρ.

Into Greek Iambics.

  YES! But this lady
Walks discontented, with her watry eyes
Bent on the earth. The unfrequented woods
Are her delight; and when she sees a bank
Stuck full of flowers, she with a sigh will tell
Her servants what a pretty place it were
To bury lovers in; and make her maids
Pluck 'em, and strew her over like a corse.

She carries with her an infectious grief,
That strikes all her beholders; she will sing
The mournful'st things that ever ear hath heard,
And sigh and sigh again; and when the rest
Of our young ladies, in their wanton blood,
Tell mirthful tales in course, that fill the room
With laughter, she will with so sad a look
Bring forth a story of the silent death
Of some forsaken virgin, which her grief
Will put in such a phrase, that ere she end,
She'll send them weeping one by one away.

Into Greek Prose.

By what right, O Athenians, is Lacedæmon our judge? Corinth may impel her into war against us; but Corinth can never place her on the judgment-seat of Greece; nor shall their united voices make us answer to the citation. We will declare not to her, but to all, our reasons and our rights. The Corcyreans had erected a trophy at Leucimna, and had spared after the victory their Corinthian captives; they had laid waste the territory of Leucas, and they had burnt the arsenal of Cyllene. Meanwhile the Corinthians sent ambassadors to every power in the Peloponnese, and enlisted mariners for their service upon every coast. If valour and skill and constancy could have availed the Corcyreans, they would have continued to abstain, as they had ever done, from all alliances. They only sought ours when destruction was imminent; knowing that, in policy and humanity, we never could allow the extinction of one Grecian state, nor consequently the aggrandisement and preponderance of another; and least so when the insolence of Corinth had threatened our naval ascendancy (by which all Greece was saved), and the rivalry of Lacedæmon our equality on land. By our treaty with the Lacedæmonians it is provided that, if any community be not in alliance with one of the parties, it may confederate with either, at its discretion; and this compact, it was agreed, should be binding, not only on the principals, but likewise on the subordinates. In such a predicament stands Corcyra.

It might behove us to chastise the inhumanity of a nation which, like Corinth, would devour her own offspring; but it certainly is most just, and most expedient, when, instead of reasoning or conferring with us on the propriety of our interference, she runs at once to Sparta, conspiring with her to our degradation, and if possible, to our ruin. Satisfactorily to demonstrate our justice and moderation, I advise that we stipulate with Corcyra for mutual defence, never for aggression, and admitting no article which, even by a forced interpretation, may contravene our treaty with Lacedæmon.

Into Latin Elegiacs.

How fearful 'tis to walk the sounding shore,
When lowers the sky, and winds are piping loud!
And round the beach the tearful maidens crowd,
Scar'd at the swelling surge, and thunder's roar.
High o'er the cliffs the screaming sea-mews soar,
Lost is th' adventurous bark in stormy cloud,
The shrill blast whistles through the fluttering shroud;
And, lo, the gallant crew, that erst before
Secure rode tilting o'er the placid wave,
Scarce know to stem the black and boisterous main,

And view with eyes aghast their watery grave.
So fares it with the breast of him, the swain,
Who quits content for mad ambition's lore;
Short are his days, and distant far the shore.

Translate TACITUS, *Annal.* II. 71, 72.

Into Latin Prose.

⊁ TRAJAN was ambitious of fame; and as long as mankind shall continue to bestow more liberal applause on their destroyers than on their benefactors, the thirst of military glory will ever be the vice of the most exalted characters. The praises of Alexander, transmitted by a succession of poets and historians, had kindled a dangerous emulation in the mind of Trajan. Like him, the Roman emperor undertook an expedition against the nations of the east; but he lamented with a sigh, that his advanced age scarcely left him any hopes of equalling the renown of the son of Philip. Yet the success of Trajan, however transient, was rapid and specious. The degenerate Parthians, broken by intestine discord, fled before his arms. He descended the river Tigris in triumph, from the mountains of Armenia to the Persian gulf. He enjoyed the honour of being the first, as he was the last of the Roman generals, who ever navigated that remote sea. His fleets ravaged the coasts of Arabia; and Trajan vainly flattered himself that he was approaching towards the confines of India.⊁ Every day the astonished senate received the intelligence of new names and new nations that acknowledged his sway. They were informed, that the kings of Bosphorus, Colchos, Iberia, Albania, Osrhoene, and even the Parthian monarch himself, had accepted their diadems from the hands of the emperor; that the independent tribes of the Median and Carduchian hills had implored his protection; and that the rich countries of Armenia, Mesopotamia, and Assyria, were reduced into the state of provinces. But the death of Trajan soon clouded the splendid prospect; and it was justly to be dreaded, that so many distant nations would throw off the unaccustomed yoke, when they were no longer restrained by the powerful hand which had imposed it. ✢

For Greek or Latin Hexameters.

WHEN the famed Argo now secure had pass'd
The crushing rocks, and that terrific strait
That guards the wintry Pontic, the tall ship
Reach'd wild Bebrycia's shores; bearing like gods
Her god-descended chiefs. They, from her sides,
With scaling steps descend, and on the shore,
Savage, and sad, and beat by ocean winds,
Strew'd their rough beds, and on the casual fire
The vessels place. The brothers, by themselves,
Castor and red-hair'd Pollux, wander far
Into the forest solitudes. A wood
Immense and dark, shagging the mountain-side,
Before them rose; a cold and sparkling fount
Well'd with perpetual lapse, beneath its feet,
Of purest water clear; scatt'ring below,
Streams, as of silver and of crystal, rose,
Bright from the bottom. Pines, of stateliest height,
Poplar, and plane, and cypress, branching wide,
Were near, thick bordered by the scented flow'rs
That lured the honey'd bee, when spring declines,
Thick swarming o'er the meadows. There all day
A huge man sat, of savage wild aspect;

His breast stood roundly forward, his broad back
Seem'd as of iron, such as might befit
A vast Colossus sculptur'd. Full to view
The muscles of his brawny shoulders stood,
Like the round mountain-stones, the torrent-wave
Has polish'd: from his neck and back hung down
A lion's skin, held by its claws. Him first
The red-hair'd youth address'd. Hail stranger, hail,
And say, what tribes unknown inhabit here.

Into Greek Prose.

THE beginning of nations, those excepted of whom sacred books have spoken, is to this unknown. Nor only the beginning, but the deeds also of many succeeding ages, yea, periods of ages, either wholly unknown, or obscured and blemished with fables. Whether it were that the use of letters came in long after, or were it the violence of barbarous inundations, or they themselves at certain revolutions of time, fatally decaying, and degenerating into sloth and ignorance; whereby the monuments of more ancient civility have been some destroyed, some lost. Perhaps disesteem and contempt of the public affairs then present, as not worth recording, might partly be in cause. Certainly oft-times we see that wise men, and of best ability, have forborne to write the acts of their own days, while they beheld with a just loathing and disdain, not only how unworthy, how perverse, how corrupt, but often how ignoble, how petty, how below all history the persons and their actions were; who either by fortune, or some rude election, had attained as a sore judgment and ignominy upon the land, to have chief sway in managing the commonwealth.

Into Latin Lyrics or Elegiacs.

Though now no more the musing ear
Delights to listen to the breeze,
That lingers o'er the greenwood shade,
  I love thee, Winter! well.

Sweet are the harmonies of Spring;
Sweet is the Summer's evening gale,
And sweet the autumnal winds that shake
  The many colour'd grove.

And pleasant to the sober'd soul
The silence of the wintry scene,
When nature shrouds herself, entranced
  In deep tranquillity.

Not undelightful now to roam
The wild heath sparkling on the sight;
Not undelightful now to pace
  The forest's ample rounds;

And see the spangled branches shine,
And mark the moss of many a hue
That varies the old tree's brown bark,
  Or o'er the grey stone spreads;

And mark the cluster'd berries bright
Amid the holly's gay green leaves;
The ivy round the leafless oak
  That clasps its foliage close.

Translate Herodotus, v. 103—5.

Into Greek Prose.

NATIONS as well as men arrive at maturity by degrees, and the events which happened during their infancy or early youth cannot be recollected, and deserve not to be remembered. The gross ignorance which anciently covered all the north of Europe, the continual migrations of its inhabitants, and the frequent and destructive revolutions which these occasioned, render it impossible to give any authentic account of the origin of the different kingdoms now established there. Everything beyond that short period to which well-attested annals reach, is obscure; an immense space is left for invention to occupy; each nation, with a vanity inseparable from human nature, hath filled that void with events calculated to display its own antiquity and lustre. History, which ought to record truth and to teach wisdom, often sets out with retailing fictions and absurdities.

Into Latin Elegiacs.

BENEATH those rugged elms, that yew tree's shade,
Where heaves the turf in many a mouldering heap,
Each in his narrow cell for ever laid,
The rude forefathers of the hamlet sleep.

The breezy call of incense-breathing morn,
The swallow twittering from the straw-built shed,
The cock's shrill clarion, or the echoing horn,
No more shall rouse them from their lowly bed.

For them no more the blazing hearth shall burn,
Or busy housewife ply her evening care:
No children run to lisp their sire's return,
Or climb his knees the envied kiss to share.

Oft did the harvest to their sickle yield,
Their furrow oft the stubborn glebe has broke;
How jocund did they drive their team afield!
How bow'd the woods beneath their sturdy stroke!

Let not ambition mock their useful toil,
Their homely joys, and destiny obscure;
Nor grandeur hear with a disdainful smile
The short and simple annals of the poor.

Into Latin Prose.

THE reformation of the senate was one of the first steps in which Augustus laid aside the tyrant, and professed himself the father of his country. He was elected censor; and, in concert with his faithful Agrippa, he examined the list of the senators, expelled a few members, whose vices or whose obstinacy required a public example, persuaded near two hundred to prevent the shame of an expulsion by a voluntary retreat, raised the qualification of a senator to about ten thousand pounds, created a sufficient number of the patrician families, and accepted for himself the honourable title of Prince of the Senate, which had always been bestowed by the censors on the citizen the most eminent for his honours and services. But whilst he thus restored the dignity, he destroyed the independence of the senate. The principles of a free constitution are irrecoverably lost, when the legislative power is nominated by the executive.

Into Latin Lyrics.

I VIEW thee on the calmy shore
When Ocean stills his waves to rest;
 Or when slow-moving on the surges hoar
 Meet with deep hollow roar
And whiten o'er his breast;
And when the moon with softer radiance gleams,
And lovelier heave the billows in her beams.

 When the low gales of evening moan along
I love with thee to feel the calm cool breeze,
 And roam the pathless forest wilds among,
Listening the mellow murmur of the trees
Full-foliaged, as they lift their arms on high,
And wave their shadowy heads in wildest melody.

 Or lead me where amid the tranquil vale
The broken stream flows on in silver light;
 And I will linger where the gale
 O'er the bank of violets sighs,
Listening to hear its soften'd sounds arise;
And hearken the dull beetle's drowsy flight,
 And watch the horn-eyed snail
 Creep o'er his long moon-glittering trail,
And mark where radiant through the night
Shines in the grass-green hedge the glow-worm's living light.

Translate THUCYDIDES, III. 112, 113.

Into Greek Prose.

POLYBIUS, reprehending Timæus for his partiality against Agathocles, whom he himself allows to be the most cruel and impious of all tyrants, says: If he took refuge in Syracuse, as asserted by that historian, flying the dirt and smoke and toil of his former profession of a porter; and if proceeding from such slender beginnings, he became master in a little time of all Sicily; brought the Carthaginian state into the utmost danger; and at last died in old age, and in possession of kingly dignity: must he not be allowed something prodigious and extraordinary, and to have possessed great talents and capacity for business and action? His historian, therefore, ought not to have alone related what tended to his reproach and infamy; but also what might redound to his praise and honor.

Translate SOPHOCLES, *Œdipus Tyrannus, from*
v. 216, αἰτεῖς, *to* v. 275, θεοί.

Into Greek Iambics.

BE they accursed!
Accursed be they in all time and place,
Accursed be they in the camp and mart,
Accursed be they in the city and field,
Accursed be their flying and abiding,
Accursed be their waking and their rest—
We curse the land that feeds them when they hunger,
We curse the arm that props them when they faint;
Withered and blasted be that hand and arm!

We curse the tongue that speaks to them, the ear
That hears them, though it be but unawares!
Blistered and cankered be that tongue and ear!
The earth in which their bodies shall be buried
We curse, except it cast their bodies out:
We shut the gates of heaven against their souls,
And as this candle that I fling to the ground,
So be their light extinguished in the pit!

For Latin Prose.

THE same Homer, who pleased at Athens and Rome two thousand years ago, is still admired at Paris and at London. All the changes of climate, government, religion, and language, have not been able to obscure his glory. Authority or prejudice may give a temporary vogue to a bad poet or orator; but his reputation will never be durable or general. When his compositions are examined by posterity, or by foreigners, the enchantment is dissipated, and his faults appear in their true colours. On the contrary, a real genius, the longer his works endure, and the more wide they are spread, the more sincere is the admiration which he meets with. Envy and jealousy have too much place in a narrow circle; and even familiar acquaintance with his person may diminish the applause due to his performances: but when these obstructions are removed, the beauties, which are naturally fitted to excite agreeable sentiments, immediately display their energy; and while the world endures, they maintain their authority over the minds of men.

Into Latin Elegiacs.

O WERE my love yon lilac fair,
    Wi' purple blossoms in the spring;
And I, a bird to shelter there,
    When wearied on my little wing:

How I wad mourn, when it was torn
    By autumn wild and winter rude!
But I wad sing on wanton wing,
    When youthfu' May its bloom renew'd.

"O gin my love were yon red rose,
    That grows upon the castle wa',
And I mysel' a drap o' dew,
    Into her bonie breast to fa'!

"Oh, there beyond expression blest,
    I'd feast on beauty a' the night;
Seal'd on her silk-saft faulds to rest,
    'Till fley'd awa' by Phœbus' light."

Translate THUCYDIDES, III. 112, 113.

For Greek Prose.

THE regency at Lacedæmon has resolved to make an irruption into Attica, if we attempt anything adverse to Potidæa; hearing that on the declaration of hostilities by Corinth, we ordered the Potidæans, whose infidelity we had detected, to demolish the wall facing Pallene. In reliance on their treason, Perdiccas and the Corinthians had entered into confederacy, and were exciting the defection of our Thracian auxiliaries. Perdiccas prevailed with the Chalcidians to dismantle all their towns upon the seaside, and to congregate in Olynthus. We made a truce, and afterwards a treaty, with Perdiccas: he evacuates the territory he had invaded; we strictly beleaguer the revolted Potidæa. The ephors of Lacedæmon now summon to appear before them not only their allies, but whosoever has any complaint to prefer against the Athenians. Thereupon the Megareans come forward and protest that they have been prohibited from our markets, contrary to treaty; and what is worse, that we exclude them from the possession of Potidæa, so convenient for extending their power and authority into Thrace. They appear, in their long oration, to have forgotten nothing, unless that they had murdered our citizens and ambassadors.

Translate SOPHOCLES, *Œdipus Tyrannus, from* v. 1369, ὡς μὲν τάδ᾽, *to* v. 1415, βροτῶν.

Into Greek Iambics.

THRICE she assayed with flattering prayers and sighs
And amorous reproaches to win from me
My capital secret, in what part my strength
Lay stor'd, in what part summ'd, that she might know:
Thrice I deluded her, and turned to sport
Her importunity, each time perceiving
How openly and with what impudence
She purpos'd to betray me, and, which was worse
Than undissembled hate, with what contempt
She sought to make me traitor to myself:
Yet the fourth time, when mustering all her wiles
With blandish'd parlies, feminine assaults,

Tongue-batteries, she decreas'd not day nor night
To storm me overwatch'd and wearied out,
At times when men seek most repose and rest,
I yielded, and unlock'd her all my heart,
Who with a grain of manhood well-resolv'd
Might easily have shook off all her snares:
But foul effeminacy held me yok'd
Her bond-slave: O indignity: O blot
To honour and religion! servile mind
Rewarded well with servile punishment!
The base degree to which I now am fall'n,
These rags, this grinding, is not yet so base
As was my former servitude, ignoble,
Unmanly, ignominious, infamous,
True slavery, and that blindness worse than this,
That saw not how degenerately I served.

For Greek Prose.

ETHELBERT, the king, to whom Austin at his landing had sent a new and wondrous message, that he came from Rome to proffer heaven and eternal happiness in the knowledge of another God than the Saxons knew, appoints them to remain where they landed, and necessaries to be provided them, consulting in the mean time what was to be done. And after certain days coming into the island, chose a place to meet them under the open sky, possest with an old persuasion, that all spells, if they should use any to deceive him, so it were not within doors, would be unavailable. They on the other side called to his presence, advancing for their standard a silver cross, and the painted image of our Saviour, came slowly forward, singing their solemn litanies: which wrought in Ethelbert more suspicion perhaps that they used enchantments; till setting down as the king will'd them, they there preached to him, and all in that assembly, the tidings of salvation. Whom having heard attentively, the king thus answered: Fair indeed and ample are the promises which ye bring, and such things as have the appearance in them of much good, yet such as being new and uncertain, I cannot hastily assent to, quitting the religion which from my ancestors, with all the English nation, so many years I have retained. Nevertheless, because ye are strangers, and have endured so long a journey to impart to us the knowledge of things which I persuade me you believe to be the truest and the best, ye may be sure we shall not recompense you with any molestation, but shall provide rather how we may friendliest entertain ye; nor do we forbid whom ye can, by preaching, gain to your belief.

Into Latin Elegiacs.

THE world's bright comforter, whose beamsome light,
Poor creatures cheereth, mounting from the deep,
His course doth in prefixed compass keep;
And as courageous giant takes delight
To run his race, and exercise his might,
Till him, down gallopping the mountain's steep,
Clear Hesperus, smooth messenger of sleep,
Views; and the silver ornament of night
Forth brings, with stars past number in her train;
All which with sun's long borrow'd splendour shine;
The seas, with full tide swelling, ebb again;
All years to their old quarters new resign;
The winds forsake their mountain-chambers wild;
And all in all things with God's virtue fill'd.

Translate LIVY, *Book* I. *Chap.* 26.

For Latin Prose.

It was a sad and solemn sight to see this train of noble ladies, and the very Volscian soldiers stood in silence as they passed by, and pitied them and honoured them. They found Caius sitting on the general's seat in the midst of the camp, and the Volscians' chiefs were standing round him. When he first saw them he wondered what it could be; but presently he knew his mother, who was walking at the head of the train; and then he could not contain himself, but leapt down from his seat, and ran to meet her, and was going to kiss her. But she stopped him and said, "Ere thou kiss me, let me know whether I am speaking to an enemy or to my son; whether I stand in thy camp as thy prisoner or as thy mother." Caius could not answer her, and then she went on, and said, "Must it be then, that had I never borne a son, Rome never should have seen the camp of an enemy? that had I remained childless, I should have died a free woman in a free city? But I am too old to bear much longer either thy shame or my misery. Rather look to thy wife and children, whom if thou persistest thou art dooming to an untimely death, or a long life of bondage." Then Virgilia and his children came up to him and kissed him, and all the noble ladies wept, and bemoaned their own fate, and the fate of their country. At last Caius cried out, "O mother, what hast thou done to me!" and he wrung her hand vehemently, and said, "Mother, thine is the victory; a happy victory for thee and for Rome, but shame and ruin to thy son." Then he fell on her neck and embraced her, and he embraced his wife and his children, and sent them back to Rome; and led away the army of the Volscians, and never afterwards attacked Rome any more; but he lived on a banished man amongst the Volscians, and when he was very old, and had neither wife nor children around him, he was wont to say, " That now in old age he knew the full bitterness of banishment." So Caius lived and died amongst the Volscians.

Into Latin Alcaics.

You who are earth, and cannot rise
    Above your sence,
Boasting the envyed wealth which lyes
Bright in your mistris' lips or eyes,
Betray a pittyed eloquence.

That which doth joyne our soules, so light
    And quieke doth move,
That like the eagle in his flight,
It doth transcend all humane sight,
Lost in the element of love.

You poets reach not this who sing
    The praise of dust,
But kneaded, when by theft you bring
The rose and lily from the spring
T' adorne the wrinckled face of lust.

When we speake love, nor art nor wit
    We glosse upon:
Our soules engender, and beget
Ideas, which you counterfeit
In your dull propagation.

While time seven ages shall disperse,
    Wee'le talke of love,
And when our tongues hold no commerse,
Our thoughts shall mutually converse;
And yet the blood no rebell prove.

And though we be of severall kind
    Fit for offence;
Yet are we so by love refined
From impure drosse, we are all mind.
Death could not more have conquer'd sence.

How suddenly those flames expire
    Which scorch our clay?
Prometheus-like, when we steale fire
From heaven, 'tis endlesse and intire;
It may know age, but not decay.

Into Greek Prose.

WHEN Pericles, the great Athenian statesman and general, was on his death-bed, his surrounding friends, deeming him now insensible, began to indulge their sorrow for their expiring patron, by enumerating his great qualities and successes, his conquests and victories, the unusual length of his administration, and his nine trophies erected over the enemies of the republic. "You forget, (cries the dying hero, who had heard all,) you forget the most eminent of my praises, while you dwell so much on those vulgar advantages, in which fortune had a principal share. You have not observed, that no citizen has ever yet worn mourning on my account."

Into Latin Elegiacs.

You meaner beauties of the night,
   That poorly satisfie our eies
More by your number, than your light;
   You common people of the skies,
   What are you when the moon shall rise?

Ye violets that first appeare,
   By your pure purple mantles known,
Like the proud virgins of the yeare,
   As if the spring were all your own;
   What are you when the rose is blown?

Ye curious chaunters of the wood,
   That warble forth dame Nature's layes,
Thinking your passions understood
   By your weak accents: what's your praise,
   When Philomell her voyce shall raise?

So when my mistris shal be seene
   In sweetnesse of her looks and minde;
By virtue first, then choyce a queen;
   Tell me, if she was not design'd
   Th' eclypse and glory of her kind.

Into Latin Prose.

The provinces of the empire (as they have been described in the preceding chapter) were destitute of any public force, or constitutional freedom. In Etruria, in Greece, and in Gaul, it was the first care of the senate to dissolve those dangerous confederacies which taught mankind, that, as the Roman arms prevailed by division, they might be resisted by union. Those princes, whom the ostentation of gratitude or generosity permitted for a while to hold a precarious sceptre, were dismissed from their thrones, as soon as they had performed their appointed task of fashioning to the yoke the vanquished nations. The free states and cities which had embraced the cause of Rome, were rewarded with a nominal alliance, and insensibly sunk into real servitude. The public authority was everywhere exercised by the ministers of the senate and of the emperors, and that authority was absolute, and without control. But the same salutary maxims of government, which had secured the peace and obedience of Italy, were extended to the most distant conquests. A nation of Romans was gradually formed in the provinces, by the double expedient of introducing colonies, and of admitting the most faithful and deserving of the provincials to the freedom of Rome.

Translate HERODOTUS, *Book* VI. *Chap.* 100.

Into Greek Prose.

THERE is nothing, perhaps, more adverse to nature and reason, than to hold in obedience remote countries and foreign nations, in opposition to their inclination and interest. A torrent of barbarians may pass over the earth, but an extensive empire must be supported by a refined system of policy and oppression: in the centre, an absolute power, prompt in action, and rich in resources; a swift and easy communication with the extreme parts; fortifications to check the first effort of rebellion; a regular administration to protect and punish; and a well-disciplined army to inspire fear, without provoking discontent and despair. Far different was the situation of the German Cæsars, who were ambitious to enslave the kingdom of Italy. Their patrimonial estates were stretched along the Rhine, or scattered in the provinces; but this ample domain was alienated by the imprudence or distress of successive princes: and their revenue, from minute and vexatious prerogative, was scarcely sufficient for the maintenance of their household. Their troops were formed by the legal or voluntary service of their feudal vassals, who passed the Alps with reluctance, assumed the licence of rapine and disorder, and capriciously deserted before the end of the campaign. Whole armies were swept away by the pestilential influence of the climate; the survivors brought back the bones of their princes and nobles; and the effects of their own intemperance were often imputed to the treachery and malice of the Italians, who rejoiced at least in the calamities of the barbarians. This irregular tyranny might contend on equal terms with the petty tyrants of Italy; nor can the people, or the reader, be much interested in the event of the quarrel.

For Latin Elegiacs.

WHAT can atone (O ever-injured shade!)
Thy fate unpitied, and thy rites unpaid?
No friend's complaint, no kind domestic tear
Pleas'd thy pale ghost, or grac'd thy mournful bier:
By foreign hands thy dying eyes were clos'd,
By foreign hands thy decent limbs compos'd,
By foreign hands thy humble grave adorn'd,
By strangers honour'd, and by strangers mourn'd!
What though no friends in sable weeds appear,
Grieve for an hour, perhaps, then mourn a year,
And bear about the mockery of woe
To midnight dances and the public show?

What though no weeping loves thy ashes grace,
Nor polish'd marble emulate thy face?
What though no sacred earth allow thee room,
Nor hallow'd dirge be mutter'd o'er thy tomb?
Yet shall thy grave with rising flowers be dress'd,
And the green turf lie lightly on thy breast:
There shall the morn her earliest tears bestow,
There the first roses of the year shall blow;
While angels with their silver wings o'ershade
The ground now sacred by thy relics made.
So peaceful rests, without a stone, a name,
What once had beauty, titles, wealth, and fame.
How lov'd, how honour'd once, avails thee not,
To whom related, or by whom begot;
A heap of dust alone remains of thee,
'Tis all thou art, and all the proud shall be!
Poets themselves must fall, like those they sung,
Deaf the prais'd ear, and mute the tuneful tongue.
Ev'n he, whose soul now melts in mournful lays,
Shall shortly want the generous tear he pays;
Then from his closing eyes thy form shall part,
And the last pang shall tear thee from my heart;
Life's idle business at one gasp be o'er,
The Muse forgot, and thou belov'd no more!

Translate SOPHOCLES, *Œdipus Coloneus, from* v. 674, εὐίππου, *to end of Chorus: into English Prose and Latin Lyrics.*

Into Latin Prose.

WHEN Augustus resolved to establish a permanent military force, for the defence of his government against foreign and domestic enemies, he instituted a peculiar treasury for the pay of the soldiers, the rewards of the veterans, and the extraordinary expences of war. The ample revenue of the excise, though peculiarly appropriate to those uses, was found inadequate. To supply the deficiency, the emperor suggested a new tax of five per cent. on all legacies and inheritances. But the nobles of Rome were more tenacious of property than of freedom. Their indignant murmurs were received by Augustus with his usual temper. He candidly referred the whole business to the senate, and exhorted them to provide for the public service by some other expedient of a less odious nature. They were divided and perplexed. He insinuated to them that their obstinacy would oblige him to propose a general land-tax and capitation. They acquiesced in silence. The new imposition on legacies and inheritances was, however, mitigated by some restrictions. It did not take place unless the object was of a certain value, most probably of fifty or an hundred pieces of gold; nor could it be exacted from the nearest kin on the father's side. When the rights of nature and poverty were thus secured, it seemed reasonable that a stranger, or a distant relation, who acquired an unexpected accession of fortune, should cheerfully resign a twentieth part of it for the benefit of the state.

Into Alcaics.

FORCE not to over-growth the subject mind:
Heaven's is the power that spread the native soil;
The tillage only asks thy careful toil,
On primal strength dependent; if confined

In depth, and barren, simple be thy seed,
Of hardy grain: God's providence hath need
Of some to marshal well the ranks behind,
As of the lofty spirits born to lead.
But if the tender plants of truth thou sow,
Let there be depth of matter genial;
And if the frosts should nip, and strong winds blow,
Their kindly opposites should countervail:
Blest gifts, unfailing in their fostering might,
Sunshine by day, the dews of heaven by night.

Translate THUCYDIDES, IV. 33—35.

Translate into Greek Prose.

AFTER these two opinions were delivered, the one most opposite to the other, the Athenians were at contention which they should decree; and at the holding up of hands, they were both sides almost equal: but yet the sentence of Diodotus prevailed. Whereupon they presently in haste sent away another galley, lest not arriving before the former, the should find the city already destroyed. The first galley set forth before the second, a day and a night. But the Mitylenian ambassadors having furnished this latter with wine and barley-cakes, and promised them great rewards if they overtook the other galley; they rowed diligently, at one and the same time both plying their oars, and taking their refection of the said barley-cakes steeped in wine and oil; and by turns part of them slept, and the other part rowed. It happened also that there blew no wind against them; and the former galley making no great haste, as going on so sad an errand, whereas the latter proceeded in the manner before mentioned, arrived indeed first, but only so much, as Paches had read the sentence, and prepared to execute what they had decreed. But presently after came in the other galley, and saved the city from being destroyed. So near were the Mitylenians to the danger.

For Greek Iambics.

WULFSTAN.

     I BID her be resolved,
Her choice now planted, forth of it to bring
The fruits of constancy: for constancy
On all things works for good: the barren breeds,
The fluent stops, the fugitive is fixed
By constancy. I told you, did I not,
The story of the wind, how he himself,
The desultory wind, was wrought upon?

OSCAR.

Yes, Sir: you told it twice.

WULFSTAN.

      Her tale was this:
The wind, when first he rose and went abroad
Through the waste region, felt himself at fault,
Wanting a voice: and suddenly to earth
Descended with a wafture and a swoop,
Where, wandering volatile, from kind to kind,
He wooed the several trees to give him one.
First he besought the ash: the voice he lent
Fitfully, with a free and lasting change,
Flung here and there its sad uncertainties:
The aspen next: a fluttered frivolous twitter
Was her sole tribute: from the willow came,

So long as dainty summer dress'd her out,
A whispering sweetness, but her winter note
Was hissing, dry, and reedy: lastly the pine
Did he solicit, and from her he drew
A voice so constant, soft, and lowly deep,
That there he rested, welcoming in her
A mild memorial of the ocean-cave
Where he was born.

Translate Livy, *Book* III. 67, 68.

Into Latin Prose.

Now might be seen a difference between the silent or downright spoken affection of some children to their parents, and the talkative obsequiousness of others; while the hope of inheritance over-acts them, and on the tongue's end enlarges their duty. Cordeilla out of mere love, without the suspicion of expected reward, at the message only of her father in distress, pours forth true filial tears. And not enduring either that her own, or any other eye should see him in such forlorn condition as his messenger declared, discreetly appoints one of her trusted servants, first to convey him privately towards some good sea-town, there to array him, bathe him, cherish him, furnish him with such attendance and state as beseemed his dignity, that then, as from his first landing, he might send word of his arrival to her husband Aganippus. Which done with all mature and requisite contrivance, Cordeilla with the king her husband, and all the barony of his realm, who then first had news of his passing the sea, go out to meet him; and after all honourable and joyful entertainment,

Aganippus, as to his wife's father, and his royal guest, surrenders him, during his abode there, the power and disposal of his whole dominion; permitting his wife Cordeilla to go with an army, and set her father upon his throne. Wherein her piety so prospered, as that she vanquished her impious sisters with those dukes; and Leir again, as saith the story, three years obtained the crown. To whom dying, Cordeilla with all regal solemnities gave burial in the town of Leicestre.

Into Elegiacs.

EPIMENIDES.

HE went into the woods a laughing boy;
Each flower was in his heart; the happy bird
Flitting across the morning sun, or heard
From way-side thicket, was to him a joy:
The water-springs, that in their moist employ
Leapt from their banks, with many an inward word
Spoke to his soul, and every leaf that stirred
Found notice from his quickly-glancing eye.
There wondrous sleep fell on him: many a year
His lids were closed: youth left him, and he woke
A careful noter of men's ways; of clear
And lofty spirit: sages, when he spoke,
Forgot their systems; and the worldly-wise
Shrunk from the gaze of truth with baffled eyes.

Translate HERODOTUS, II. 73.

Into Greek Prose.

The outlaw, being for his many crimes and villanies banished from the towns and houses of honest men, and wandering in waste places, far from danger of law, maketh his mantle his house, and under it covereth himself from the wrath of heaven, from the offence of the earth, and from the sight of men. When it raineth, it is his penthouse; when it bloweth, it is his tent; when it freezeth, it is his tabernacle. In summer he can wear it loose; in winter he can wrap it close; at all times, he can use it; never heavy, never cumbersome. Likewise for a rebel it is as serviceable: for in this war that he maketh (if at least it deserve the name of war) when he still flieth from his foe, and lurketh in the thick woods, and strait passages, waiting for advantages, it is his bed, yea, and almost his household-stuff. For the wood is his house against all weathers, and his mantle is his couch to sleep in: therein he wrappeth himself round, and coucheth himself strongly against the gnats, which in that country do more annoy the naked rebels, whilst they keep the woods, and do more sharply wound them, than all their enemies' swords or spears, which can seldom come nigh them. Yea, and oftentimes their mantle serveth them, when they are near driven, being wrapped about their left arm, instead of a target; for it is hard to cut through with a sword; besides, it is light to bear, light to throw away, and being (as they commoly are) naked, it is to them all in all. Lastly for a thief, it is so handsome, as it may seem it was first invented for him: for under it he may cleanly convey any fit pillage that cometh handsomely in his way; and when he goeth abroad in the night in free-booting, it is his best and surest friend; for lying, as they often do, two or three nights together abroad, to watch for their booty, with that they can prettily shroud themselves under a bush or a bank-side, till they can conveniently do their errand: and when all is over, he can in his mantle pass through any town or company being close hooded over his head, as he useth, from knowledge of any to whom he is endangered.

Into Latin Elegiacs.

TO THE REVEREND SHADE OF HIS RELIGIOUS FATHER.

THAT for seven lusters I did never come
To doe the rites to thy religious tombe:
That neither haire was cut, or true teares shed
By me, or thee, as justments to the dead:
Forgive, forgive me: since I did not know
Whether thy bones had here their rest or no.
But now 'tis known, behold, behold, I bring
Unto thy ghost th' effused offering:
And look, what smallage, nightshade, cypresse, yew,
Unto the shades have been, or now are due,
Here I devote: and something more then so:
I come to pay a debt of birth I owe.
Thou gav'st me life, but mortal: for that one
Favour I'll make full satisfaction!
For my life mortall, rise from out thy herse,
And take a life immortall from my verse.

For Latin Hexameters.

There is a poor blind man, who every day,
In summer sunshine, or in winter's rain,
Duly as tolls the bell, to the high fane
Explores, with faltering footsteps, his dark way,
To kneel before his Maker, and to hear
The chanted service, pealing full and clear.
Ask why, alone, in the same spot he kneels
Through the long year? Oh! the wide world is cold
As dark to him. Here he no longer feels
His sad bereavement. Faith and hope uphold
His heart. He feels not he is poor and blind,
Amid the unpitying tumult of mankind:
As through the aisles the choral anthems roll,
His soul is in the choirs above the skies,
And songs far off, of angel-companies,
When this dim earth is perish'd as a scroll.
Oh! happy if the rich, the vain, the proud,
The plumed actors in life's motley crowd,
Since pride is dust, and life itself a span,
Would learn one lesson from a poor blind man.

Into Latin Prose.

Titus Antoninus Pius has been justly denominated a second Numa. The same love of religion, justice, and peace, was the distinguishing characteristic of both princes. But the situation of the latter opened a much larger field for the exercise of those virtues. Numa could only prevent a few neighbouring villagers from plundering each other's harvests. Antoninus diffused order and tranquillity over the greatest part of the earth. His reign is marked by the rare advantage of furnishing very few materials for history; which is, indeed, little more than the register of the crimes, follies, and misfortunes of mankind. In private life, he was an amiable as well as a good man. The native simplicity of his virtue was a stranger to vanity or affectation. He enjoyed, with moderation, the conveniences of his fortune, and the innocent pleasures of society; and the benevolence of his soul displayed itself in a cheerful serenity of temper.

Into Greek Iambics.

We have not time to mourn.

      The worse for us!
He that lacks time to mourn, lacks time to mend,
Eternity mourns that. 'Tis an ill cure
For life's worst ills, to have no time to feel them.
Where sorrow's held intrusive, and turned out,
There wisdom will not enter, nor true power,
Nor aught that dignifies humanity.
Yet such the barrenness of busy life!
From shelf to shelf Ambition clambers up,
To reach the naked'st pinnacle of all,
Whilst Magnanimity, absolved from toil,
Reposes self-included at the base.

For Latin Prose.

Whenever he appeared in the streets and public places of Constantinople, Belisarius attracted and satisfied the eyes of the people. His lofty stature and majestic countenance fulfilled their expectations of an hero; the meanest of his fellow-citizens were emboldened by his gentle and gracious demeanour; and the martial train which attended his foot-steps, left his person more accessible than in a day of battle. Seven thousand horsemen, matchless for beauty and valour, were maintained in the service, and at the private expense, of the general. Their prowess was always conspicuous in single combats, or in the foremost ranks; and both parties confessed, that in the siege of Rome, the guards of Belisarius had alone vanquished the barbarian host. Their numbers were continually augmented by the bravest and most faithful of the enemy; and his fortunate captives, the Vandals, the Moors, and the Goths, emulated the attachment of his domestic followers.

Translate HORACE, *Book* III. *Ode 5.*

Into Latin Alcaics.

ARION.

Not song, nor beauty, nor the wondrous power
Of the clear sky, nor stream, nor mountain-glen,
Nor the wide ocean, turn the hearts of men
To love, nor give the world-embracing dower
Of inward gentleness: up from the bed
Blest by chaste beauty, men have risen to blood,
And life hath perished in the flow'ry wood,
And the poor traveller beneath starlight bled.
Thus that musician, in his wealth of song
Pouring his numbers, even with the sound
Swimming around them, would the heartless throng
Have thrust into his death; but with a bound
Spurning the cursed ship, he sought the wave,
And nature's children did her poet save.

Into Greek Prose.

THERE is very little ground, either from reason or observation, to conclude the world eternal or incorruptible. The continual and rapid motion of matter, the violent revolutions with which every part is agitated, the changes remarked in the heavens, the plain traces as well as tradition of an universal deluge, or general convulsion of the elements; all these prove strongly the mortality of this fabric of the world, and its passage, by corruption or dissolution, from one state or order to another. It must, therefore, as well as each individual form which it contains, have its infancy, youth, manhood, and old age; and it is probable, that, in all these variations, man, equally with every animal and vegetable, will partake. In the flourishing age of the world, it may be expected, that the human species should possess greater vigour both of mind and body, more prosperous health, higher spirits, longer life, and a stronger inclination and power of generation. But if the general system of things, and human society of course, have any such gradual revolutions, they are too slow to be discernible in that short period which is comprehended by history and tradition. Stature and force of body, length of life, even courage and extent of genius, seem hitherto to have been naturally, in all ages, pretty much the same. The arts and sciences, indeed, have flourished in one period, and have decayed in another. But we may observe, that, at the time when they rose to greatest perfection among one people, they were perhaps totally unknown to all the neighbouring nations; and though they universally decayed in one age, yet in a succeeding generation they again revived, and diffused themselves over the world. As far, therefore, as observation reaches, there is no universal difference discernible in the human species; and though it were allowed, that the universe, like an animal body, had a natural progress from infancy to old age; yet as it must still be uncertain whether at present it be advancing to its point of perfection, or declining from it, we cannot thence pre-suppose any decay in human nature. To prove, therefore, or account for the greater populousness of antiquity, by the imaginary youth, or vigour of the world, will scarcely be admitted by any just reasoner.

Into Latin Elegiacs.

Sun-begotten, Ocean-born,
Sparkling in the summer-morn
Underneath me as I pass,
O'er the hill-top on the grass,
All among thy fellow-drops
On the speary herbage-tops,
Round, and bright, and warm, and still,
Over all the northern hill;—
Who may be so blest as thee,
Of the sons of men that be?
Evermore thou dost behold
All the sun-set bathed in gold;
Then thou listenest all night long
To the leaves' faint under song,
From two tall dark elms, that rise
Up against the silent skies:
Evermore thou drink'st the stream
Of the chaste moon's purest beam;
Evermore thou dost espy
Every star that twinkles by;

Till thou hearest the cock crow
From the barton* far below;
Till thou seest the dawn-streak
From the eastern night-clouds break;
Till the mighty king of light
Lifts his unsoiled visage bright,
And his speckled flocks has driven
To batten in the fields of heaven;
Then thou lightest up thy breast
With the lamp thou lovest best;
Many rays of one thou makest,
Giving three for one thou takest;
Love and constancy's best blue,
Sunny warmth of golden hue,
Glowing red, to speak thereby
Thine affection's ardency:—
Thus rejoicing in his might,
Made a creature of his light,
Thou art all content to be
Lost in his immensity;
And the best that can be said,
When they ask why thou art fled,
Is, that thou art gone to share
With him the empire of the air.

Into Latin Prose.

THERE is a prevailing maxim, among some reasoners, that every new tax creates a new ability in the subjects to bear it, that each increase of public burdens increases proportionably

---

* Farm-yard.

the industry of the people. This maxim is of such a nature as is most likely to be abused; and is so much the more dangerous, as its truth cannot be altogether denied: but it must be owned, when kept within certain bounds, to have some foundation in reason and experience. When a tax is laid upon commodities which are consumed by the common people, the necessary consequence may seem to be, either that the poor must retrench something from their way of living, or raise their wages, so as to make the burden of the tax fall entirely upon the rich. But there is a third consequence, which often follows upon taxes, viz. that the poor increase their industry, perform more work, and live as well as before, without demanding more for their labour. Where taxes are moderate, are laid on gradually, and affect not the necessaries of life, this consequence naturally follows; and it is certain, that such difficulties often serve to excite the industry of a people, and render them more opulent and laborious than others who enjoy the greatest advantages.

Into Latin Alcaics.

If thou wouldst find what holiest men have sought,
Communion with the power of poesy,
Empty thy mind of all unquiet thought,
Lay bare thy spirit to the vaulting sky
And glory of the sunshine: go and stand
Where nodding briers sport with the water-break,
Or by the plashings of a moonlight creek;
Or breast the wind upon some jutting land:
The most unheeded things have influences
That sink into the soul; in after hours

We oft are tempted suddenly to dress
The tombs of half-forgotten moods with flowers:
Our own choice mocks us; and the sweetest themes
Come to us without call, wayward as dreams.

Translate VIRGIL, *Æn.* IV. 173—218.

Into Latin Hexameters.

OF Brian's birth strange tales were told:
His mother watch'd a midnight fold,
Built deep within a dreary glen,
Where scatter'd lay the bones of men,
In some forgotten battle slain,
And bleach'd by drifting wind and rain.
It might have tamed a warrior's heart,
To view such mockery of his art!
The knot-grass fetter'd there the hand,
Which once could burst an iron band;
Beneath the broad and ample bone
That buckler'd heart to fear unknown,
A feeble and a timorous guest,
The field-fare framed her lowly nest;
There the slow blind-worm left his slime
On the fleet limbs that mock'd at time;
And there, too, lay the leader's skull,
Still wreath'd with chaplet, flush'd and full,
For heath-bell with her purple bloom,
Supplied the bonnet and the plume.

Translate THUCYDIDES, I. 5.

Into Greek Prose.

THE original station allotted to man by his Creator was in the mild and fertile regions of the East. There the human race began its career of improvement; and from the remains of sciences which were anciently cultivated, as well as of arts which were anciently exercised in India, we may conclude it to be one of the first countries in which men made any considerable progress in that career. The wisdom of the East was early celebrated, and its productions were early in request among distant nations. The intercourse, however, between different countries was carried on at first entirely by land. As the people of the East appear soon to have acquired complete dominion over the useful animals, they could early undertake the long and toilsome journeys which it was necessary to make, in order to maintain this intercourse; and by the provident bounty of heaven, they were furnished with a beast of burden, without whose aid it would have been impossible to accomplish them. The camel, by its persevering strength, by its moderation in the use of food, and the singularity of its internal structure, which enables it to lay in a stock of water sufficient for several days, put it in their power to convey bulky commodities through those deserts, which must be traversed by all who travel from any of the countries west of the Euphrates towards India. Trade was carried on in this manner, particularly by the nations near to the Arabian Gulf, from the earliest period to which historical information reaches. Distant journeys, however, would be taken at first only occasionally, and by a few adventurers. But by degrees, from attention to their mutual safety and comfort, numerous bodies of merchants assembled at stated times, and, forming a temporary association, known afterwards by the name of a caravan, governed by officers of their own choice, and subject to regulations of which experience had taught them the utility, they performed journeys of such extent and duration, as appear astonishing to nations not accustomed to this mode of carrying on commerce.

Into Latin Elegiacs or Greek Iambics.

Now the third and fatal conflict of the Persian throne is done,
And the Moslem's fiery valour has the crowning victory won.
Harmosan, the last and boldest the invaders to defy,
Captive, overborne by numbers, they are bringing forth to die.
Then exclaimed that noble captive—" Lo! I perish in my thirst.
Give me but one drink of water, and let then arrive the worst."
In his hand he took the goblet, but awhile the draught forbore,
Seeming doubtfully the purpose of the foeman to explore.
Well might then have paused the bravest, for around him angry foes
With an hedge of naked weapons did that lonely man enclose.
"But what fear'st thou?" cried the caliph: "is it, friend, a secret blow?
Fear it not—our gallant horsemen no such treacherous dealing know.
Thou may'st quench thy thirst securely, for thou shalt not die before
Thou hast drunk that cup of water—this reprieve is thine—no more."
Quick the satrap dashed the goblet down to earth with ready hand,
And the liquid sank for ever, lost amid the burning sand.

"Thou hast said that mine my life is, till the water of that cup
I have drained—then bid thy servants that spilled water
  gather up."
For a moment stood the caliph, as by doubtful passions
  stirred,
Then exclaimed, "For ever sacred must remain a monarch's
  word!
Bring another cup, and straightway to the noble Persian give:
Drink, I said before, and perish—now I bid thee drink, and
  live."

TRENCH.

Into Latin Prose.

At the distance of a mile from the capital, in the field of Mars, before the palace of Hebdomon, the troops halted; and the emperor, as well as his minister, advanced, according to ancient custom, respectfully to salute the power which supported their throne. As Rufinus passed along the ranks, and disguised with studied courtesy his innate haughtiness, the wings insensibly wheeled from the right and left, and enclosed the devoted victim within the circle of their arms. Before he could reflect on the danger of his situation, Gainas gave the signal of death; a daring and forward soldier plunged his sword into the breast of the guilty prefect; and Rufinus fell, groaned, and expired, at the feet of the affrighted emperor. If the agonies of a moment could expiate the crimes of a whole life, or if the outrages inflicted on a breathless corpse could be the object of pity, our humanity might perhaps be affected by the horrid circumstances which accompanied the murder of Rufinus. His mangled body was abandoned to the brutal fury of the populace of either sex, who hastened in crowds, from every quarter of the city, to trample on the remains of the haughty minister, at whose frown they had so lately trembled. His right hand was cut off, and carried through the streets of Constantinople, in cruel mockery, to extort contributions for the avaricious tyrant, whose head was publicly exposed, borne aloft on the point of a long lance.

Into Latin Alcaics.

✢ The glories of our birth and state
    Are shadows, not substantial things:
There is no armour against fate;
    Death lays his icy hand on kings.
        Sceptre and crown
        Must tumble down,
And in the dust be equal made
With the poor crooked scythe and spade.

Some men with swords may reap the field,
    And plant fresh laurels where they kill;
But their strong nerves at last must yield;
    They tame but one another still.
        Early or late,
        They stoop to fate,
And must give up their murmuring breath,
When they, pale captives, creep to death.

The garlands wither on your brow,
    Then boast no more your mighty deeds;
Upon death's purple altar now,
    See where the victor victim bleeds.
        All heads must come
        To the cold tomb;
Only the actions of the just
Smell sweet, and blossom in the dust. ✢

Into Greek Prose.

God, whom the wisest men acknowledge to bee a Power uneffable, and Vertue infinite, a Light by abundant charitie invisible, and Understanding which itselfe can onely comprehend, an Essence eternall and spirituall, of absolute purenesse and simplicity; was, and is pleased to make himselfe knowne by the worke of the world: in the wonderfull magnitude whereof (all which He imbraceth, filleth, and sustaineth) we behold the image of that glory which cannot be measured, and withall that one, and yet universall Nature, which cannot be defined. In the glorious lights of Heaven we perceive a shadow of his divine countenance; in his mercifull provision for all that live, his manifold goodnesse; and lastly, in creating and making existent the world universall, by the absolute art of his owne word, his power and almightinesse; which Power, Light, Vertue, Wisdom, and Goodnesse, being all but attributes of one simple essence, and one God, we in all admire, and in part discerne, *per speculum creaturarum*, that is, in the disposition, order, and variety of celestiall and terrestriall bodies: terrestriall, in their strange and manifold diversities; celestiall, in their beauty and magnitude; which in their continuall and contrary motions are neither repugnant, intermixt, nor confounded. By these potent effects we approach to the knowledge of the omnipotent cause, and by these motions, their Almighty Mover.

Into Latin Elegiacs.

We want but little: in the morning-tide,
    Bread to renew our energies; at noon,
Cool shade, to quiet evening yielding soon;
    And then a ramble by the hedge-row side,

Or what our cottage embers can provide
Of social comfort; and at night, the boon
Of peaceful slumber, when the gleamy moon
Up the lone heavens in starry state doth ride.
All that is more than these, into our life
By accident of place or station brought,
Feeds not the silent growth of ripening thought,
Wisdom best learned apart from throngs and strife,
In the broad fields, the sky's unvalued wealth,
And seasons gliding past us in their stealth.

Into Latin Prose.

THE siege of Petra, which the Roman general, with the aid of the Lazi, immediately undertook, is one of the most remarkable actions of the age. The city was seated on a craggy rock, which hung over the sea, and communicated by a steep and narrow path with the land. Since the approach was difficult, the attack might be deemed impossible: the Persian conqueror had strengthened the fortifications of Justinian; and the places least inaccessible were covered by additional bulwarks. In this important fortress the vigilance of Chosroes had deposited a magazine of offensive and defensive arms, sufficient for five times the number, not only of the garrison, but of the besiegers themselves. The stock of flour and salt provisions was adequate to the consumption of five years; the want of wine was supplied by vinegar, and of grain, from whence a strong liquor was extracted; and a triple aqueduct eluded the diligence, and even the suspicions, of the enemy. But the firmest defence of Petra was placed in the valour of fifteen hundred Persians, who resisted the assaults of the Romans, whilst, in a softer vein of earth, a mine was secretly perforated. The wall, supported by slender and temporary props, hung tottering in the air; but Dagisteus delayed the attack till he had secured a specific recompense; and the town was relieved before the return of his messenger from Constantinople. The Persian garrison was reduced to four hunded men, of whom no more than fifty were exempt from sickness or wounds; yet such had been their inflexible perseverance, that they concealed their losses from the enemy, by enduring, without a murmur, the sight and putrefying stench of the dead bodies of their eleven hundred companions. After their deliverance, the breaches were hastily stopped with sand-bags; the mine was replenished with earth; a new wall was erected on a frame of substantial timber; and a fresh garrison of three thousand men was stationed at Petra to sustain the labours of a second siege. The operations, both of attack and defence, were conducted with skilful obstinacy; and each party derived useful lessons from the experience of their past faults. A battering-ram was invented, of light construction and powerful effect: it was transported and worked by the hands of forty soldiers; and as the stones were loosened by its repeated strokes, they were torn with long iron hooks from the wall. From those walls a shower of darts was incessantly poured on the heads of the assailants, but they were most dangerously annoyed by a fiery composition of sulphur and bitumen, which in Colchos might with some propriety be named the oil of Medea. Of six thousand Romans who mounted the scaling-ladders, their general, Bessas, was the first, a gallant veteran of seventy years of age: the courage of their leader, his fall, and extreme danger, animated the irresistible effort of his troops; and their prevailing numbers oppressed the strength, without subduing the spirit, of the Persian garrison. The fate of these valiant men deserves to be more distinctly noticed. Seven hundred had perished in the siege, two thousand three hundred survived to defend the breach. One thousand and seventy were destroyed with fire and sword in the last assault; and if seven hundred and thirty were made prisoners, only eighteen among them were found without the marks of honourable wounds. The remaining five hundred escaped into the citadel, which they maintained without any hopes of relief, rejecting the fairest terms of capitulation and service, till they were lost in the flames. They died in obedience to the commands of their prince; and such examples of loyalty and valour might excite their countrymen to deeds of equal despair and more prosperous event. The instant demolition of the works of Petra confessed the astonishment and apprehension of the conqueror.

Into Greek Iambics.

MESSENGER.

O WHITHER shall I run, or which way fly
The sight of this so horrid spectacle,
Which erst my eyes beheld, and yet behold?
For dire imagination still pursues me.
But providence or instinct of nature seems,
Or reason though disturbed, and scarce consulted,
To have guided me aright, I know not how,
To thee first, reverend Manoah, and to these
My countrymen, whom here I knew remaining,
As at some distance from the place of horror,
So in the sad event too much concern'd.

MANOAH.

The accident was loud, and here before thee
With rueful cry, yet what it was we hear not;
No preface needs, thou seest we long to know.

MESSENGER.

It would burst forth, but I recover breath,
And sense distract, to know well what I utter.

MANOAH.

Tell us the sum, the circumstance defer.

MESSENGER.

Gaza yet stands, but all her sons are fall'n,
All in a moment overwhelm'd and fallen.

MANOAH.

Sad; but thou know'st to Israelites not saddest
The desolation of a hostile city.

MESSENGER.

Feed on that first, there may in grief be surfeit.

MANOAH.

Relate by whom?

MESSENGER.

By Samson.

MANOAH.

That still lessens
The sorrow, and converts it nigh to joy.

MESSENGER.

Ah! Manoah, I refrain too suddenly
To utter what will come at last too soon;
Lest evil tidings with too rude irruption
Hitting thy aged ear should pierce too deep.

MANOAH.

Suspense in news is torture, speak them out.

MESSENGER.

Take then the worst in brief, Samson is dead.

MANOAH.

All by him fell thou say'st, by whom fell he?
What glorious hand gave Samson his death's wound?

MESSENGER.

Unwounded of his enemies he fell.

MANOAH.

Wearied with slaughter then, or how? explain.

MESSENGER.

By his own hands.

MANOAH.

    Self-violence? what cause
Brought him so soon at variance with himself
Among his foes?

MESSENGER.

    Inevitable cause,
At once both to destroy and be destroy'd;
The edifice, where all were met to see him,
Upon their heads and on his own he pull'd.

MANOAH.

O lastly over-strong against thyself!
A dreadful way thou took'st to thy revenge.
More than enough we know: but, while things yet
Are in confusion, give us, if thou can'st,
Eye-witness of what first or last was done,
Relation more particular and distinct.

MESSENGER.

Occasions drew me early to this city,
And as the gates I entered with sun-rise,
The morning trumpet's festival proclaim'd
Through each high street. Little I had dispatch'd
When all abroad was rumour'd, that this day
Samson should be brought forth to show the people
Proof of his mighty strength in feats and games.
I sorrow'd at his captive state, but minded
Not to be absent at that spectacle.

The building was a spacious theatre,
Half round, on two main pillars vaulted high,
With seats, where all the lords and each degree
Of sort might sit in order to behold;
The other side was open, where the throng
On banks and scaffolds under sky might stand;
I among these aloof obscurely stood.
The feast and noon grew high, and sacrifice
Had fill'd their hearts with mirth, high cheer, and wine,
When to their sports they turn'd. Immediately
Was Samson as a public servant brought,
In their state livery clad; before him pipes
And timbrels, on each side went armed guards,
Both horse and foot, before him and behind,
Archers, and slingers, cataphracts, and spears.
At sight of him the people with a shout
Rifted the air, clamouring their god with praise,
Who had made their dreadful enemy their thrall.
He patient, but undaunted, where they led him,
Came to the place, and what was set before him,
Which without help of eye might be assay'd
To heave, pull, draw, or break, he still perform'd,
All with incredible stupendous force,
None daring to appear antagonist.
At length for intermission sake they led him
Between the pillars; he his guide requested,
For so from such as nearer stood we heard,
As over-tir'd to let him lean awhile
With both his arms on those two massy pillars,
That to the arched roof gave main support.
He unsuspicious led him; which, when Samson
Felt in his arms, with head awhile inclin'd,
And eyes fast fixt he stood, as one who pray'd,

Or some great matter in his mind revolv'd:
At last with head erect thus cried aloud,
Hitherto, lords, what your commands impos'd
I have perform'd, as reason was, obeying,
Not without wonder, or delight beheld:
Now of my own accord such other trial
I mean to show you of my strength, yet greater;
As with amaze shall strike all who behold.
This utter'd, straining all his nerves he bow'd,
As with the force of winds and waters pent,
When mountains tremble, those two massy pillars
With horrible confusion to and fro,
He tugg'd, he shook, till down they came, and drew
The whole roof after them, with burst of thunder
Upon the heads of all who sat beneath,
Lords, ladies, captains, counsellors, or priests,
Their choice nobility and flower, not only
Of this, but each Philistian city round,
Met from all parts to solemnize this feast.
Samson, with these immixt, inevitably
Pull'd down the same destruction on himself;
The vulgar only scap'd who stood without.

Into Greek Prose.

Many tyrants have beene changed into worthy kings: and many have ill used their ill-gotten dominion, which, becomming hereditary to their posterity, hath grown into the most excellent forme of government, even a lawfull monarchy. But they that live under a tyrannicall citie, have no such hope: their mistresse is immortall, and will not slacken the reines, untill they be pulled out of her hands, and her owne mouth receive the bridle of a more mightier chariotter. This is wofull: yet their present sufferings make them lesse mindefull of the future New flies and hungry ones, fall upon the same sore, out of which others had already sucked their fill. A new governour comes yearely among them, attended by all his poore kindred and friends, who meane not to returne home empty to their hives, without a good lading of waxe and hony. These flie into all quarters, and are quickly acquainted with every man's wealth, or whatsoever else, in all the province, is worthy to be desired. They know all a man's enemies, and all his feares: becomming themselves within a little space the enemies that he feareth most. To grow into acquaintance with these masterfull guests, in hopes to win their friendship, were an endlesse labour (yet it must be undergone), and such as every one hath not means to goe about: but were this effected, what continually inflames the tyrant's appetite, and will not suffer it to be restrained with any limits of respect. Why should he seek out bounds to prescribe unto his desires, who cannot endure the face of one so honest, as may put him in remembrance of any moderation? It is much that he hath gotten by extorting from some few: by sparing none, he should have riches in goodly abundance. He hath taken a great deale from every one: but every one could have spared more. He hath wrung all their purses, and now he hath enough, but (as covetousnesse is never satisfied) he thinks that all this is too little for a stock, though it were indeed a good yearly income. Therefore he deviseth new tricks of robbery, and is not better pleased with the gains than with the art of getting. He is hated for this, and he knows it well; but he thinkes by cruelty to change hatred into feare. So he makes it his exercise to torment and murder all whom he suspecteth, in which course if he suspect none unjustly, he may be said to deale craftily; but if innocencie be not safe, how can all this make any conspirator to stand in feare, since the traitor is no worse rewarded than the quiet man? Wherefore he can think upon none other securitie, than to disarm all his subjects; to fortifie himselfe within some strong place; and, for defence of his person and state, to hire as many lustie souldiers as shall be thought sufficient. These must not be of his owne countrie: for if not every one, yet some one or other may chance to have a feeling of the public miserie. This considered, he allures unto him a desperate rabble of strangers, the most unhonest that can be found; such as have neither wealth nor credit at home, and will therefore be careful to support him, by whose only favour they are maintained. Now, lest any of these, either by detestation of his wickednesse, or (which in wicked men is most likely) by promise of greater reward than he doth give, should be drawn to turn his sword against the tyrant himselfe; they shall all be permitted to doe as he doth; to rob, to ravish, to murder, and to satisfie their owne appetites, in most outrageous maner; being thought so much the more assured to their master by how much the more he sees them grow hateful to all men else. Considering in what age, and in what language I write, I must be faine to say that these are not dreams: though some Englishmen perhaps that were unacquainted with history, lighting upon this leafe, might suppose this discourse to be but little better. This is to shew, both how tyrannie growes to stand in need of mercenarie souldiers, and how those mercenaries are, by mutuall obligation, firmly assured unto the tyrant.

Into Latin Elegiacs.

Two friends, or brothers, with devout intent,
On some far pilgrimage together went.
It happen'd so that, when the sun was down,
They just arriv'd by twilight at a town:
That day had been the baiting of a bull,
'Twas at a feast, and every inn so full
That no void room in chamber or on ground,
And but one sorry bed was to be found;
And that so little it would hold but one,
Though till this hour they never lay alone.
So were they forc'd to part; one stay'd behind,
His fellow sought what lodging he could find:
At last he found a stall where oxen stood,
And that he rather chose than lie abroad.
'Twas in a farther yard without a door;
But, for his ease, well litter'd was the floor.
His fellow, who the narrow bed had kept,
Was weary, and without a rocker slept;
Supine he snor'd; but in the dead of night
He dreamt his friend appear'd before his sight,
Who, with his ghastly look, and doleful cry,
Said, Help me, brother, or this night I die;
Arise and help before all help be vain,
Or in an ox's stall I shall be slain.
Rous'd from his rest, he waken'd in a start,
Shivering with horror, and with aching heart;
At length to cure himself by reason tries;
'Tis but a dream, and what are dreams but lies?
So thinking, chang'd his side and clos'd his eyes.
His dream returns: his friend appears again:
The murderers come, now help, or I am slain:
'Twas but a vision still, and visions are but vain.

He dreamt the third: but now his friend appear'd
Pale, naked, pierced with wounds, with blood besmear'd:
Thrice warn'd, awake, said he, relief is late,
The deed is done: but thou revenge my fate:
Tardy of aid, unseal thy heavy eyes,
Awake, and with the dawning day arise;
Take to the western gate thy ready way,
For by that passage they my corpse convey:
My corpse is in a tumbril laid, among
The filth and ordure, and inclos'd with dung:
That cart arrest, and raise a common cry:
For sacred hunger of my gold I die:
Then shew'd his grisly wound: and last he drew
A piteous sigh, and took a long adieu.
The frighted friend arose by break of day,
And found the stall where late his fellow lay.
Then of his impious host inquiring more,
Was answer'd that his guest was gone before;
Muttering, he went, said he, by morning-light,
And much complain'd of his ill rest by night.
This rais'd suspicion in the pilgrim's mind,
Because all hosts are of an evil kind,
And oft, to share the spoils, with robbers join'd.
His dream confirm'd his thought: with troubled look,
Straight to the western gate his way he took;
There, as his dream foretold, a cart he found,
That carry'd compost forth to dung the ground.
This, when the pilgrim saw, he stretch'd his throat,
And cry'd out murder with a yelling note.
My murder'd fellow in this cart lies dead,
Vengeance and justice on the villain's head.
Ye magistrates, who sacred laws dispense,
On you I call to punish the offence.

The word thus giv'n, within a little space
The mob came roaring out, and throng'd the place.
All in a trice they cast the cart to ground,
And in the dung the murder'd body found:
Though breathless, warm, and reeking from the wound.
Good heaven, whose darling attribute we find,
Is boundless grace, and mercy to mankind,
Abhors the cruel: and the deeds of night
By wonderous ways reveals in open light:
Murder may pass unpunish'd for a time,
But tardy justice will o'ertake the crime.
And oft a speedier pain the guilty feels:
The hue and cry of Heaven pursues him at the heels.
Fresh from the fact, as in the present case,
The criminals are seiz'd upon the place:
Carter and host confronted face to face.
Stiff in denial, as the law appoints,
On engines they distend their tortur'd joints:
So was confession forc'd, th' offence was known,
And public justice on th' offenders done.

Into Latin Hexameters.

THE oracles are dumb,
No voice or hideous hum
   Runs through the arched roof in words deceiving.
Apollo from his shrine
Can no more divine,
   With hollow shriek the steep of Delphos leaving.
No nightly trance, or breathed spell
Inspires the pale-ey'd priest from the prophetic cell.

The lonely mountains o'er,
And the resounding shore,

A voice of weeping heard and loud lament;
From haunted spring, and dale
Edg'd with poplar pale,
   The parting genius is with sighing sent;
With flow'r-inwoven tresses torn,
The nymphs in twilight shade of tangled thickets mourn.

In consecrated earth,
And on the holy hearth,
   The Lars and Lemures moan with midnight plaint;
In urns, and altars round,
A drear and dying sound
   Affrights the Flamens at their service quaint;
And the chill marble seems to sweat,
While each peculiar pow'r forgoes his wonted seat.

Nor war, or battle-sound
Was heard the world around:
   The idle spear and shield were high up hung,
The hooked chariot stood
Unstained with hostile blood,
   The trumpet spake not to the armed throng,
And kings sat still with awful eye,
As if they surely knew their sov'reign Lord was by.

But peaceful was the night,
Wherein the Prince of Light,
   His reign of peace upon the earth began:
The winds with wonder whist
Smoothly the waters kist,
Whisp'ring new joys to the mild ocean,
Who now hath quite forgot to rave,
While birds of calm sit brooding on the charmed wave.

The stars with deep amaze
Stand fix'd in steadfast gaze,

Bending one way their precious influence,
And will not take their flight,
For all the morning light,
　　Or Lucifer that often warn'd them thence;
But in their glimmering orbs did glow,
Until their Lord himself bespake, and bid them go.

And though the shady gloom
Had given day her room,
　　The sun himself withheld his wonted speed,
And hid his head for shame,
As his inferior flame
　　The new enlightened world no more should need;
He saw a greater Sun appear
Than his bright throne, or burning axletree could bear.

The shepherds on the lawn,
Or e'er the point of dawn,
　　Sat simply chatting in a rustic row;
Full little thought they then
That the mighty Pan
　　Was kindly come to live with them below;
Perhaps their loves, or else their sheep,
Was all that did their silly thoughts so busy keep.

When such music sweet
Their hearts and ears did greet,
　　As never was by mortal finger strook,
Divinely-warbled voice
Answering the stringed noise,
　　As all their souls in blissful rapture took:
The air, such pleasure loath to lose,
With thousand echoes still prolongs each heavenly close.

THE END.

LIST OF CLASSICAL WORKS,

RECENTLY PUBLISHED BY

J. & J. J. DEIGHTON,

Agents to the University,

CAMBRIDGE.

Æschylus.
Græce, recensuit J. SCHOLEFIELD, A.M., Coll. SS. Trin. nuper Socius, et Græcarum Literarum Professor Regius. Editio secunda, 8vo. 12s.

Æschylus.
Appendix ad editionem Cantabrigiensem novissimam. Confecit J. SCHOLEFIELD, A.M., &c. 8vo. 1s. 6d.

Æschylus. Eumenides.
Recensuit et illustravit J. SCHOLEFIELD, A.M., &c. 8vo. 4s. 6d.

ΑΙΣΧΥΛΟΥ ΙΚΕΤΙΔΕΣ.
Æschyli Supplices. Recensuit, emendavit, explanavit, FREDERICUS A. PALEY, A.M., Coll. Div. Joh. Cant. 8vo. 6s.

ΑΙΣΧΥΛΟΥ ΟΡΕΣΤΕΙΑ.
Agamemnon, Choephori, Eumenides. Recensuit, et brevibus notis instruxit, FREDERICUS A. PALEY, A.M., Coll. Div. Joh. Cant. 8vo. 7s. 6d.
The Plays separately:
Agamemnon....................4s.
Choephori ....3s. 6d.
Eumenides ....3s. 6d.

Æschylus. Prometheus Vinctus.
The Text of DINDORF, with Notes compiled and abridged by J. GRIFFITHS, A.M., Fellow of Wadham College, Oxford. 8vo. 5s.

Æschylus. Septem Contra Thebas.
The Text of DINDORF, with Notes compiled and abridged by J. GRIFFITHS, A.M., Fellow of Wadham College, Oxford. 8vo. 5s.

Ainsworth's Dictionary.
An abridgement of, designed for the use of Schools. By THOMAS MORELL, D.D. A new edition materially improved. By JOHN CAREY, LL.D. 8vo. 12s. bound.

Alford (Rev. H.) ΠΡΟΓΥΜΝΑΣΜΑΤΑ.
Passages in Prose and Verse from English Authors for translation into Greek and Latin; together with selected Passages from Greek and Latin Authors for translation into English: forming a regular course of Exercises in Classical Composition. 8vo. cloth, 6s.

Aristophanis Acharnenses.
Recensuit et interpretatus est F. H. BLAYDES, M.A. Ædis Christi apud Oxonienses nuper Alumnus. 8vo. 7s. 6d.

Including a Critical Discussion of some Questions of Literary History connected with his works. By J. W. BLAKESLEY, M.A., Fellow and Tutor of Trinity College, Cambridge. 8vo. 8s. 6d.

Arundines Cami.
Sive Musarum Cantabrigiensium Lusus Canori; collegit atque edidit H. DRURY, A.M. Editio altera, 8vo. 12s.

Cambridge Classical Examinations.
A Collection of Questions, &c., proposed to Candidates for Classical Honours from 1810 to 1823. By a late REGIUS PROFESSOR OF GREEK. Second Edition, 8vo. 4s. 6d.

Castle (Thomas). A Table for finding the Commence-
ments, Characteristics, and Regular Inflexions of GREEK VERBS. 4to. 2s. 6d.

Demosthenes.
Select Private Orations, after the Text of DINDORF; with the various readings of REISKE and BEKKER. With English Notes, for the use of Schools. By C. T. PENROSE, A.M., Head Master of the Grosvenor School, Bath. 12mo. cloth, 5s.

ΔΗΜΟΣΘΕΝΟΥΣ Ο ΗΕΡΙ ΤΗΣ ΠΑΡΑΠΡΕΣΒΕΙΑΣ
ΛΟΓΟΣ. Demosthenis de falsa Legatione. A New Edition, with a careful revision of the Text, Annotatio Critica, English explanatory Notes, Philological and Historical, and Appendices. By RICHARD SHILLETO, M.A., Trinity College, Cambridge. 8vo. 10s. 6d.

Demosthenes.
Translation of Select Speeches, with Notes. By C. R. KENNEDY, A.M., Fellow of Trinity College. 12mo. 9s.

Dobree (Prof.) Adversaria, &c. edente J. Scholefield,
A.M., Græc. Prof. Reg. 2 vols. 8vo. 15s.

Vol. I. Containing Notes on the Greek Historians, Orators, Philosophers, &c.

Vol. II. On the Greek Tragedians, Aristophanes, Athenæus, the New Testament, and Latin writers; with Notes on Inscriptions, the Lexicon Rhetoricum, &c.

The following may be had separately:—
Adversaria, vol. I. part 1, 6s.
... vol. I. part 2, 5s.
... vol. II. part 2, 10s.
Lexicon Rhetoricum Cantabrigiense, 1s. 6d.
Miscellaneous Notes on Inscriptions, 4s.

Donaldson (Rev. J. W.) The New Cratylus, or Con-
tributions towards a more accurate knowledge of the Greek Language. 8vo. 17s.

Donaldson (Rev. J. W.) Varronianus.
A Critical and Historical Introduction to the Philological Study of the Latin Language. 8vo. 10s. 6d.

Donaldson (Rev. J. W.) Constructionis Græcæ Præ-
cepta in usum Scholarum. 12mo. cloth, 2s. 6d.

Elmsleiana Critica.
Sive Annotationes in Heracleidas, Medeam, et Bacchas. Selegit suisque et aliorum notis illustravit F. E. GRETTON, A.M., Head Master of Stamford Grammar School, 8vo. 7s. 6d.

Euripides.
Tragœdiæ quatuor, cum notis PORSONI. Recensuit, suasque notulas subjecit, J. SCHOLEFIELD, A.M., &c. Editio secunda, 8vo. 14s.

Euripides. Iphigenia in Aulide.
"Effutire leves indigna Tragœdiæ versus." Cambridge Edition, 8vo. 8s.

Euripides. Iphigenia in Tauris.
Cambridge Edition, 8vo. 5s.

Hephæstion. Concerning Metres and Poems.
Translated into English, and illustrated by Notes and a Rhythmical Notation; with Prolegomena on Rhythm and Accent. By T. F. BARHAM, M.B. 8vo. 8s. 6d.

Herodotus.
Codicem SANCROFTI manuscriptum denuo contulit reliquam lectionis varietatem commodius digessit annotationes variorum adjecit THOMAS GAISFORD, S.T.P. Editio altera, 2 vols. 8vo. 1l. 1s.

Horatius.
Ad fidem Textus R. BENTLEII, plerumque emendata et brevibus notis instructus. Edidit T. KIDD, A.M. 8vo. large paper, 9s.

Livy. The History of Rome.
By C. W. STOCKER, D.D., late Fellow of St John's College, Oxford. Vol. I. Part 1. 8vo. 12s., Vol. II. Parts 1 and 2. 1l. 4s.

Maltby (Bp.) A new and complete Greek Gradus, or
Poetical Lexicon of the Greek Language, with a Latin and English Translation, &c. Second Edition, 8vo. 1l. 1s.

Philological Museum.
2 vols. 8vo. 1l. 10s. *Each of the six Numbers contained in the 2 vols. may be had separately, 5s.*

Pindar. Epinician or Triumphal Odes, in four books,
together with the Fragments of his lost compositions. Revised and explained by J. W. DONALDSON, A.M., Head Master of Bury School. 8vo. 16s.

Plato. Schleiermacher's Introductions to the Dialogues.
Translated from the German by W. DOBSON, A.M., Fellow of Trinity College. 8vo. 12s. 6d.

Plautus. Aulularia.
Notis et Glossario locuplete instruxit. J. HILDYARD, A.M., Coll. Christi apud Cantab. Socius. Editio altera, 8vo. 7s. 6d.

Plautus. Menæchmei.
Notis et Glossario locuplete instruxit. J. HILDYARD, A.M., Coll. Christi apud Cantab. Socius. Editio altera, 8vo. 7s. 6d.

Seale (Dr.) An Analysis of the Greek Metres.
For the use of Students at the Universities. Tenth Edition, 8vo. 3s. 6d.

Sophocles.
With Notes Critical and Explanatory, adapted to the use of Schools and Universities. By T. MITCHELL, A.M., late Fellow of Sidney Sussex College, Cambridge. 2 vols. 8vo. cloth, 1l. 8s.,
Or the Plays separately:

Œdipus Tyrannus. 8vo. 7s. | Electra. 8vo. 5s.
Œdipus Coloneus. 8vo. 5s. | Trachiniæ. 8vo. 5s.
Antigone. 8vo. 5s. | Philoctetes. 8vo. 5s.
Ajax. 8vo. 5s.

Tacitus.
Historiæ ex editione Brotier. Locis Annalium ab eo citatis, selectis et additis, quibusdam etiam notis subjunctis, ab editore R. RELHAN, A.M., 8vo. 12s.

Tacitus. De Moribus Germanorum, et de Vita Agricolæ,
ex editione G. BROTIER, curâ R. RELHAN, A.M., &c. *With Maps of Ancient Britain and Germany.* Editio quarta, 12mo. 5s. 6d.

Terentius.
Ex recensione F. Lindenbrogii, cum notis variorum, Scholiis, et Index Verborum et Phrasium. Edidit J. A. GILES, A.M., &c. 8vo. 9s.

Theatre of the Greeks.
A series of papers relating to the History and Criticism of the Greek Drama. With a new Introduction and other alterations. By J. W. DONALDSON, A.M., Head Master of Bury St Edmund's Grammar School. Fifth Edition, 8vo. 15s.

Thucydides.
Græce, ex recensione Bekkeri. 8vo. 14s.

ΘΟΥΚΥΔΙΔΗΣ. The History of the Peloponnesian
War, by Thucydides: Illustrated by Maps, taken entirely from actual Surveys. With Notes, chiefly Historical and Geographical. By THOMAS ARNOLD, D.D. 3 vols. 8vo. Second Edition, 1l. 10s.

Virgilius.
Notis ex editione Heyniana excerptis illustrata. Accedit index Maittairianus. 8vo. 14s.

LIST OF THEOLOGICAL WORKS,

RECENTLY PUBLISHED BY

J. & J. J. DEIGHTON,

Agents to the University,

CAMBRIDGE.

Η ΚΑΙΝΗ ΔΙΑΘΗΚΗ ΜΕΤΑ ΥΠΟΜΝΗΜΑΤΩΝ ΑΡΧΑΙΩΝ, ΕΚΔΙΔΟΜΕΝΗ ΥΠΟ ΘΕΟΚΛΗΤΟΥ ΦΑΡΜΑΚΙΔΟΥ. The New Testament, with the Commentaries of Euthymius, Œcumenius, Arethas, &c. Edited by the Rev. THEOCLITUS PHARMAKIDES, Professor of Theology and Greek Literature in the Royal University of Athens, &c. Vols. I. to IV., comprising the Gospels, the Acts, and the Epistles to the Romans and Corinthians. 4 vols. 8vo. 1*l*. 18*s*.

Acts of the Apostles.
With Notes original and selected. For the use of Students in the University. By HASTINGS ROBINSON, D.D., formerly Fellow of St John's College, Cambridge. 8vo. 8*s*.

Altar Service.
With the Rubricks, &c. in Red. Royal 4to.
In Sheets .... 0 12*s*.
Calf, lettered and Registers........................ 1 1 0

Bibles, Prayer Books, and Church Services, printed at the University Press, in a variety of bindings.

Blunt (Professor). Sketch of the Church of the first
Two Centuries after Christ, drawn from the Writings of the Fathers, down to Clemens Alexandrinus inclusive. 8vo. 6*s*. 6*d*.

Blunt (Professor). An Introduction to a Course of
Lectures on the Early Fathers, now in delivery in the University of Cambridge. Parts I. and II. 8vo. 2*s*. each.

Bushby (Rev. E.) Introduction to the Study of the
Holy Scriptures. Fourth Edition, 12mo. 3*s*. 6*d*.

Bushby (Rev. E.) Essay on the Human Mind.
Fourth Edition, 12mo. 3*s*. 6*d*.

Butler (Bp.) A Summary of the Argument on his
Analogy of Religion. 8vo. 1*s*.

Butler (Bp.) An Analysis of his Three Sermons on
Human Nature, and his Dissertation on Virtue. With a concise Summary of his System of Morals. 12mo. 1*s*.

Cheke (Sir John). Translation of the Gospel according to St Matthew, and part of the first Chapter of the Gospel according to St Mark, with original Notes. Also VII Original Letters of Sir J. Cheke. Prefixed is an Introductory Account of the nature and object of the Translation. By J. GOODWIN, B.D., Fellow and Tutor of Corpus Christi College, Cambridge. 8vo. 7s. 6d.

Chrysostomi (S. Joannis). Homiliæ in Mattheum. Textum ad fidem codicum MSS. et versionum emendavit, præcipuam lectionis varietatem adscripsit, annotationibus ubi opus erat, et novis indicibus instruxit F. FIELD, A.M., Coll. SS. Trin. Socius. 3 vols. 8vo. 2l. 2s. Large Paper, 4l. 4s.

Cruden (Alex.) A complete Concordance of the Old and New Testament; with a Life of the Author. By ALEX. CHALMERS. 4to. Portrait, 1l. 1s.

Ecclesiæ Anglicanæ Vindex Catholicus, sive Articulorum Ecclesiæ Anglicanæ cum Scriptis SS. Patrum nova Collatio, cura G. W. HARVEY, A.M. Coll. Regal. Socii. 8vo. Vol. I. 16s. Vol. II. 16s. Vol. III. 19s.

Fisk (Rev. G.) Sermons preached in the Parish Church of St Botolph, Cambridge. 8vo. 10s. 6d.

Frere (Rev. John). The Doctrine of Imposition of Hands; or Confirmation the ordained and ordinary means for conveying the Gift of the Holy Ghost. 12mo. cloth, 3s. 6d.

Garrick. Mode of Reading the Liturgy of the Church of England. A New Edition, with Notes and a Preliminary Discourse. By R. CULL, Tutor in Elocution. 8vo. 5s. 6d.

Gibson (Rev. J.) Four Sermons preached before the University of Cambridge in 1837. 8vo. 1s. 6d.

Gospels. Questions on the Four Gospels, and the Acts of the Apostles, Critical, Historical, and Geographical. 12mo. 3s. 6d.

Hare (Archd.) Sermons preacht in Herstmonceaux Church. 8vo. 12s.

Hey (Prof.) Lectures in Divinity. Delivered in the University of Cambridge. Third Edition, 2 vols. 8vo. 1l. 10s.

Hildyard (Rev. J.) Five Sermons on the Parable of the Rich Man and Lazarus, preached before the University of Cambridge. To which is added a proposed Plan for the Introduction of a Systematic Study of Theology in the University. 8vo. 5s.

Hildyard (Rev. J.) Sermons, chiefly practical.

Hook (Rev. Walter Farquhar). Ecclesiastical Biography, alphabetically arranged, containing the Lives of ancient Fathers, and modern Divines, interspersed with brief notices of Heretics and Schismatics. 12mo.

This work is published in monthly parts price sixpence, each part containing 60 pages.

Hulsean Lectures.

Alford (Rev. H.) For the Year 1841.
The Consistency of the Divine Conduct in Revealing the Doctrines of Redemption. To which are added Two Sermons preached before the University of Cambridge. 8vo. 7s.

Alford (Rev. H.) For the Year 1842.
The Consistency of the Divine Conduct in Revealing the Doctrines of Redemption. Part the Second. 8vo. 6s.

Chevalier (Rev. T.) For the Year 1826.
On the Historical Types contained in the Old Testament. 8vo. 12s.

Chevalier (Rev. T.) For the Year 1827.
On the Proofs of Divine Power and Wisdom derived from the study of Astronomy; and on the Evidence, Doctrines, and Precepts of Revealed Religion. 8vo. 12s.

Howarth (Rev. H.) For the Year 1836.
Jesus of Nazareth the Christ of God. 8vo. 5s. 6d.

Howarth (Rev. H.) For the Year 1835.
The Truth and Obligation of Revealed Religion considered with reference to Prevailing Opinions. 8vo. 5s. 6d.

Rose (Rev. Henry John). For the Year 1833.
The Law of Moses viewed in connexion with the History and Character of the Jews. 8vo. 8s.

Smith (Rev. Theyre T.) For the Year 1840.
The Christian Religion in connexion with the Principles of Morality. 8vo. 7s. 6d.

Hulsean Essays.

Davies (Rev. John). For the Year 1842.
On the Relation in which the moral precepts of the Old and New Testaments stand to each other. 8vo. cloth, 3s. 6d.

Ellicott (C. J.) For the Year 1843.
The History and Obligation of the Sabbath. 8vo. sewed, 3s. 6d.

Gruggen (F. J.) For the Year 1844.
The Lawfulness and Obligation of Oaths. 8vo. sewed, 3s. 6d.

Jukes (Andrew). For the Year 1840.
An enquiry into the Principles of Prophetic Interpretation and the practical results arising from them. 8vo. cloth, 6s. 6d.

Woodhouse (Rev. Charles Wright). For the Year 1841.
The use and value of the Writings of the Ancient Fathers, considered as auxiliary to the proof of the truth of the Christian Religion, and to the elucidation of its Doctrines. 8vo. boards, 4s.

ספר זכרון The Jewish Chronicle, 4to.
Annual Subscription, 6s. For six months, 3s. 6d.

Jones (Rev. W. of Nayland). An Essay on the Church.
12mo. 1s. 6d.

Leighton (Arch.) Prælectiones Theologicæ;
Paræneses, et Meditationes in Psalmos IV. XXXII. CXXX. Ethico-Criticæ. Editio nova iterum recensente J. SCHOLEFIELD, A.M., Græc. Lit. apud Cantab. Professore Regio. 8vo. 8s. 6d.

Liturgiæ Britannicæ;
Or the several Editions of the Book of Common Prayer of the Church of England, from its compilation to the last revision; together with the Liturgy set forth for the use of the Church of Scotland; arranged to shew their respective variations. By W. KEELING, B.D., Fellow of St John's College. 8vo. 1l. 1s. The Rubrics in these Liturgies are printed in red.

Margaret, Countess of Richmond and Derby, and Foundress of Christ's and St John's Colleges, Cambridge. The Funeral Sermon, preached by BISHOP FISHER in 1509; with BAKER's Preface to the same, &c. Edited by J. HYMERS, D.D., Fellow of St John's College; with illustrative Notes, Additions, and an Appendix. 8vo. 7s. 6d.

Masson's Apology for the Greek Church; or Hints towards the Religious Improvement of the Greek Nation. Edited by J. S. HOWSON, M.A., Trinity College, one of the Masters of the Liverpool Collegiate Institution. 12mo. 2s. 6d.

Merivale (Rev. C.) The Church of England a Faithful Witness of CHRIST; not Destroying the Law, but Fulfilling it. Four Sermons preached before the University of Cambridge in 1838. 8vo. 4s.

Merivale (Rev. C.) Sermons preached in the Chapel Royal at Whitehall. 8vo. 10s. 6d.

Middleton (Dr. T. F.) The Doctrine of the Greek Article applied to the Criticism and Illustration of the New Testament. With Prefatory Observations and Notes. By HUGH JAMES ROSE, B.D. 8vo. 13s.

Mill (Dr. W. H.) Observations on the attempted Application of PANTHEISTIC Principles to the Theory and Historic Criticism of the GOSPEL. 8vo. 6s. 6d.

Mill (Dr. W. H.) The Historical Character of St Luke's first Chapter, vindicated against some recent Mythical Interpreters. 8vo. 4s.

Mill (Dr. W. H.) The Evangelical Accounts of the Descent and Parentage of the Saviour, vindicated against some recent Mythical Interpreters. 8vo. 4s.

Mill (Dr. W. H.) The Accounts of our Lord's Brethren in the New Testament vindicated against some recent Mythical Interpreters. 8vo. 4s.

Mill (Dr. W. H.) The Historical Character of the Circumstances of our Lord's Nativity in the Gospel of St Matthew vindicated against some recent Mythical Interpreters. 8vo. 4s.

Mill (Dr. W. H.) Prælectio Theologica in Scholis Cantabrigiensibus habita Kal. Feb. A. D. 1843. 4to. 2s.

Mill (Dr. W. H.) Five Sermons on the Temptation of Christ our Lord in the Wilderness. Preached before the University of Cambridge in Lent 1844. 8vo. 6s. 6d.

Mill (Dr. W. H.) Sermons preached in Lent 1845, and on several former occasions, before the University of Cambridge. 8vo. 12s.

Moore (Rev. Daniel). Sermons preached before the University of Cambridge in December 1844. 8vo. cloth, 4s.

Neale (Rev. J. M.) Ayton Priory, or the Restored Monastery. 12mo. 4s.

Norrisian Essays.

Beaufort (Rev. D. A.) For the year 1840.
Scripture sufficient without Tradition, or the Doctrine of the Sixth Article of the British Churches maintained. 8vo. sewed, 4s. 6d.

Howson (John Saul). For the year 1841.
Both in the Old and New Testaments, eternal Life is offered to mankind through Jesus Christ only. 8vo. sewed, 2s.

Woolley (Rev. Joseph). For the year 1843.
The writings of the New Testament afford indications that this portion of the Sacred Canon was intended to be a complete record of Apostolical Doctrine. 8vo. sewed, 2s.

Woolley (Rev. Joseph). For the year 1844.
"By one offering Christ hath perfected for ever them that are sanctified." Heb. x. 14. 8vo. sewed, 2s.

Offices of the Church, with the Rubrics, &c. in Red. Crown 8vo. sheets, 2s. black calf, 5s.

Paley. Analysis of the Principles of Moral and Political

Paley. Analysis of the Evidences of Christianity.
By S. FENNELL, M.A., &c. 12mo. 2s. 6d.

Paley. Examination Questions on the Evidences of Christianity. 12mo. 2s. 6d.

Parkhurst's Greek and English Lexicon to the New Testament, with additions by the late HUGH JAMES ROSE. A new edition carefully revised by J. R. MAJOR, D.D. King's College, London. 8vo. 1l. 4s.

Pearson (Bp.) Exposition of the Creed.
An Analysis of, with some additional matter occasionally interspersed. By W. H. MILL, D.D., Chaplain to the Archbishop of Canterbury. 8vo. 5s.

Preston (Theodore). קהלת.

The Hebrew Text and a Parallel Latin Version of the Book of Solomon, called Ecclesiastes; divided into the Sections adopted by R. Moses Mendlessohn, with a Literal Translation from the Rabbinic of his Commentary and Preface, and Original Notes, Philological and Exegetical. Also a New and Improved English Version of the same, similarly arranged, with Introductory Analysis of the Sections; to which is prefixed a preliminary Dissertation on the scope and Author of the Book, and various writers of eminence, who have quoted or illustrated it. 8vo. cloth, 15s.

Robinson (Professor). The Character of St Paul the Model of the Christian Ministry. Four Sermons preached before the University of Cambridge in 1840. 8vo. 3s.

Rose (Rev. Hugh James). Christianity always Progressive. 8vo. 8s. 6d.

Scholefield (Professor). Hints for an Improved Translation of the New Testament. Second edition, 8vo. 4s.

Scholefield (Professor). Scriptural Grounds of Union, considered in Five Sermons preached before the University of Cambridge in 1840. Second edition, 8vo. 3s. 6d.

Sedgwick (Professor). A Discourse on the Studies of the University. Fourth edition, 8vo. 4s.

Smith (Rev. C.) Seven Letters on National Religion. Addressed to the Rev. Henry Melville, M.A. 8vo. 7s. 6d.

Smyth (Prof.) Evidences of Christianity.
12mo. cloth, 5s.

Taylor (Bp. Jeremy). His Whole Works, with a Life

Taylor (Bp. Jeremy). Holy Living and Dying, together with Prayers. Containing the whole Duty of a Christian. 8vo. 12s.

Taylor (Bp. Jeremy). Rule and Exercises of Holy Living. 8vo. 4s.

Taylor (Bp. Jeremy). Rule and Exercises of Holy Dying. 8vo. 4s.

Tertullian. The Apology.
With English Notes and a Preface, intended as an Introduction to the study of Patristical and Ecclesiastical Latinity. By H. A. WOODHAM, A.M., Fellow of Jesus College, Cambridge. 8vo. 8s. 6d.

Thomas a Becket.
Sanctus Thomas Cantuariensis, ed. J. A. GILES, LL.D. Eccles. Anglic. Presbyter et Colleg. C. C. Oxon. olim Socius. 8 vols. 8vo. 4l. 16s. (forming vols. XXXVI. to XLIII. of Patres Ecclesiæ Anglicanæ.) This is a most complete collection of the original contemporary biographies of Thomas a Becket, by Edward Grim, Herbert de Bosham, William Fitz Stephen, Benedict of Peterborough, and many others, all of whom either knew Becket personally, and saw his death, or were in one manner or another connected with his history: together with 1000 Letters now first brought together. 6 vols. of this important and interesting collection are now first printed from MSS. Only 250 copies printed.

Thorp (Archd.) Four Sermons, preached before the University of Cambridge in May 1838. 8vo. 3s. 6d.

Turton (Dean). Natural Theology considered with reference to Lord Brougham's Discourse on that subject. Second Edition, 8vo. 8s.

Turton (Dean). The Roman Catholic Doctrine of the Eucharist considered, in reply to Dr. Wiseman's Argument from Scripture. 8vo. 8s. 6d.

Turton (Dean). Observations on Dr. Wiseman's Reply to Dr. Turton's Roman Catholic Doctrine of the Eucharist considered. 8vo. 4s. 6d.

Turton (Dean). A Vindication of the Literary Character of Professor Porson from the Animadversions of Bishop Burgess, on 1 John v. 7. By CRITO CANTABRIGIENSIS. 8vo. 11s.

Usher (Archbp.) Answer to a Jesuit.
With other Tracts on Popery. 8vo. 13s. 6d.

Welchman. Articuli Ecclesiæ Anglicanæ.
Textibus sacræ Scripturæ et Patrum Primævorum Testimoniis confirmati, brevibusque notis illustrati. Appendicis loco nunc primum adjiciuntur Catechismus Edvardi VI. et Articuli A.D. 1552 approbati. 8vo. 6s. 6d.

Wilson (Rev. Wm.) An Illustration of the Method of Explaining the New Testament by the early Opinions of the Jews and Christians concerning Christ. New Edition, 8vo. 8*s*.

Catalogue of English and Foreign Theology, and Ecclesiastical History; comprising the Holy Scriptures in various Languages, Liturgies, Fathers of the Church, &c. 8vo. 1*s*. *Allowed to Purchasers.*

LIST OF MATHEMATICAL WORKS,

RECENTLY PUBLISHED BY

J. & J. J. DEIGHTON,

Agents to the University,

CAMBRIDGE.

Airy (Astronomer Royal). Mathematical Tracts; on the Lunar and Planetary Theories; the Figure of the Earth; Precession and Nutation; the Calculus of Variations; the Undulatory Theory of Optics. Third Edition. 8vo. Plates, 15s.

Astronomical Observations, made at the Observatory of Cambridge.

By Professor Airy.			By Professor Challis.		
Vol. I. for	1828, 4to.	12s.	Vol. IX. for 1836, 4to.		1l. 5s.
Vol. II. ...	1829,	12s.	Vol. X. ... 1837,		1l. 11s. 6d.
Vol. III. ...	1830,	14s. 6d.	Vol. XI. ... 1838,		2l. 2s.
Vol. IV. ...	1831,	14s. 6d.	Vol. XII. ... 1839,		1l. 11s. 6d.
Vol. V. ...	1832,	15s.	Vol. XIII. ...	1840,	2l. 12s. 6d.
Vol. VI. ...	1833,	15s.		1841,	
Vol. VII. ...	1834,	15s.			
Vol. VIII. ...	1835,	15s.			

Booth (Rev. James). On the Rectification and Quadrature of the Spherical Ellipse. 8vo. 2s.

Booth (Rev. James). On the application of a new Analytic method to the theory of Curves and curved surfaces. 8vo. 2s. 6d.

Brooke (C.) A Synopsis of the Principal Formulæ and Results of Pure Mathematics. 8vo. 15s.

Browne (Rev. A.) A Short View of the First Principles of the Differential Calculus. 8vo. 9s.

Cambridge Philosophical Society, (Transactions of). 4to. Plates.

Vol. I.	Part 1,	1l.	Vol. V.	Part 2,	14s.
Vol. I.	Part 2,	1l. 10s.	Vol. V.	Part 3,	12s.
Vol. II.	Part 1,	18s.	Vol. VI.	Part 1,	13s.
Vol. II.	Part 2,	18s.	Vol. VI.	Part 2,	13s.
Vol. III.	Part 1,	1l. 11s. 6d.	Vol. VI.	Part 3,	13s.
Vol. III.	Part 2,	2s. 6d.	Vol. VII.	Part 1,	7s. 6d.
Vol. III.	Part 3,	3s.	Vol. VII.	Part 2,	7s.
Vol. IV.	Part 1,	15s.	Vol. VII.	Part 3,	13s.
Vol. IV.	Part 2,	1l. 1s.	Vol. VIII. Part 1,		12s.
Vol. IV.	Part 3,	12s.	Vol. VIII. Part 2,		8s. 6d.
Vol. V.	Part 1,	10s.			

Cambridge Problems;
being a Collection of the Questions proposed to the Candidates for the Degree of Bachelor of Arts, from 1811 to 1820 inclusive. 8vo. 5s.

Carnot (M.) Reflexions on the Metaphysical Principles of the Infinitesimal Analysis. Translated from the French. 8vo. 3s.

Coddington (Rev. H.) Treatise on the Reflexion and Refraction of Light. Being Part I. of a System of Optics. 8vo. Plates, 15s.

Coddington (Rev. H.) Treatise on the Eye, and on Optical Instruments. Being Part II. of a System of Optics. 8vo. Plates, 5s.

Coddington (Rev. H.) Introduction to the Differential Calculus on Algebraic Principles. 8vo. 2s. 6d.

Colenso (Rev. J. W.) Elements of Algebra, designed for the use of Schools. Fourth Edition. 12mo. 4s. 6d.

Colenso (Rev. J. W.) Arithmetic, designed for the use of Schools. Second Edition. 12mo. 4s. 6d.

Conic Sections, the Elements of the, with the Sections of Conoids. Third Edition. 8vo. 4s. 6d.

Cumming (Professor). Manual of Electro-Dynamics, chiefly translated from the French of J. F. DEMONFERRAND. 8vo. Plates, 12s.

Earnshaw (Rev. S.) Dynamics, or a Treatise on Motion; to which is added, a short Treatise on Attractions. Third Edition. 8vo. Plates, 14s.

Earnshaw (Rev. S.) Treatise on Statics, containing the Theory of the Equilibrium of Forces; and numerous Examples illustrative of the general Principles of the Science. Third Edition enlarged. 8vo. Plates, 10s.

Euclid; the Elements of.
By R. SIMSON, M.D. Twenty-fifth Edition, revised and corrected. 8vo. 8s.; 12mo. 5s.

Euclid; the Elements of.
From the Text of Simson. Edited, in the Symbolical form, by R. BLAKELOCK. 12mo. 6s.

Euclid; the Elements of. (The first three books.)
Translated from the Latin of the Right Rev. Thomas Elrington, D.D. late Lord Bishop of Leighlin and Ferns, formerly Provost of Trinity College, Dublin. To which is added a Compendium of Algebra. Designed for the use of Schools and private instruction. 12mo. 3s. 6d.

Euclid; a Companion to.
With a

Fennell (Rev. S.) Elementary Treatise on Algebra.
8vo. 9s.

regory (D. F.) Examples on the Processes of the Differential and Integral Calculus. 8vo. Plates, 18s.

regory (D. F.) Treatise on the Application of Analysis to Solid Geometry. Commenced by D. F. GREGORY, M.A., late Fellow and Assistant Tutor of Trinity College, Cambridge; concluded by W. WALTON, M.A., Trinity College, Cambridge. 8vo. cloth, 10s. 6d.

riffin (W. N.) Treatise on Optics.
Second Edition. 8vo. Plates, 8s.

Hamilton (H. P.) Principles of Analytical Geometry.
8vo. Plates, 14s.

Hewitt (Rev. D.) Problems and Theorems of Plane Trigonometry. 8vo. 6s.

Hind (Rev. J.) The Elements of Algebra.
Fifth Edition. 8vo. 12s. 6d.

Hind (Rev. J.) Introduction to the Elements of Algebra. Second Edition. 12mo. 5s.

Hind (Rev. J.) Principles and Practice of Arithmetic.
Fourth Edition. 12mo. 4s. 6d.

Hind (Rev. J.) Key to Arithmetic.
The Solutions of the Questions attended with any difficulty in the Principles and Practice of Arithmetic; with an Appendix, consisting of Questions for Examination in all the rules of Arithmetic. 8vo. 5s.

Hind (Rev. J.) Elements of Plane and Spherical Trigonometry. Fourth Edition. 12mo. 7s. 6d.

Hutton (Dr.) Mathematical Tables.
Edited by OLYNTHUS GREGORY. Royal 8vo.

Hymers (Dr.) Elements of the Theory of Astronomy.
Second Edition. 8vo. Plates, 14s.

Hymers (Dr.) Treatise on Analytical Geometry of Three Dimensions. Second Edition. 8vo. 10s. 6d.

Hymers (Dr.) Treatise on the Integral Calculus.
Third Edition. 8vo. Plates, 10s. 6d.

Hymers (Dr.) Treatise on the Theory of Algebraical Equations. Second Edition. 8vo. Plates, 9s. 6d.

H ⸻ ⸻ Treati

Hymers (Dr.) Treatise on Trigonometry, and on th
Trigonometrical Tables of Logarithms. Second Edition. 8vo. Plates 8s. 6d.

Hymers (Dr.) Treatise on Spherical Trigonometry.
8vo. Plates, 2s. 6d.

Hymers (Dr.) Treatise on Conic Sections and the Ap
plication of Algebra to Geometry. Third Edition. 8vo. 9s.

Integral Calculus;
A Collection of Examples on the. 8vo. 5s. 6d.

Jarrett (Rev. T.) An Essay on Algebraical Develop-
ment; containing the principal Expansions in Common Algebra, in the Differential and Integral Calculus, and in the Calculus of Finit Differences. 8vo. 8s. 6d.

Kelland (Rev. P.) Theory of Heat.
8vo. 9s.

Mechanical Problems,
Adapted to the course of Reading pursued in the University of Cam bridge. 8vo. 7s.

Miller (Prof.) The Elements of Hydrostatics and
Hydrodynamics Third Edition. 8vo. Plates, 6s.

Miller (Prof.) Elementary Treatise on the Differentia
Calculus. Third Edition. 8vo. Plates, 6s.

Miller (Prof.) Treatise on Crystallography.
8vo. Plates, 7s. 6d.

Miller (Prof.) Table of Mineralogical Series;
Being a Syllabus of the Lectures on Mineralogy. 8vo. 1s. 6d.

Murphy (Rev. R.) Elementary Principles of the Theory
of Electricity. 8vo. 7s. 6d.

Myers (C. J.) Elementary Treatise on the Differential
Calculus. 8vo. 2s. 6d.

Newton's Principia.
The first three Sections of Newton's Principia, with an Appendix and the ninth and eleventh Sections. Edited by JOHN H. EVANS M.A., late Fellow of St Jobn's College and Head Master of Sedbergh Grammar School. Third Edition. 8vo. 6s.

O'Brien (Rev. M.) Mathematical Tracts.
On LA PLACE's Coefficients; the Figure of the Earth; the Motion of Rigid Body about its Centre of Gravity; Precession and Nutation 8vo. 4s. 6d.

O'Brien (Rev. M.) Elementary Treatise on the Differential Calculus. 8vo. Plates, 10s. 6d.

O'Brien (Rev. M.) Treatise on Plane Co-ordinate Geometry; or the Application of the Method of Co-ordinates to the Solution of Problems in Plane Geometry. 8vo. Plates, 9s.

Peacock (Dean). Treatise on Algebra.
Vol I. Arithmetical Algebra. 8vo. 15s.
Vol. II. Symbolical Algebra, and its Applications to the Geometry of Position. 8vo. 16s. 6d.

Statics (Elementary);
Or a Treatise on the Equilibrium of Forces in One Plane. 8vo. Plates, 4s. 6d.

Stevenson (R.) Treatise on the Nature and Properties of Algebraic Equations. Second Edition. 8vo. 6s. 6d.

Trigonometry.
A Syllabus of a Course of Lectures upon, and the Application of Algebra to Geometry. Second Edition. 7s. 6d.

Walton (William). Treatise on the Differential Calculus, 8vo. cloth, 10s. 6d.

Webster (T.) The Theory of the Equilibrium and Motion of Fluids. 8vo. Plate, 9s.

Whewell (Dr.) Elementary Treatise on Mechanics. Sixth Edition, with Supplement. 8vo. Plates, 8s.

Whewell (Dr.) The Mechanical Powers:
A Supplement to the sixth edition of the Elementary Treatise on Mechanics. 8vo. 1s.

Whewell (Dr.) On the Free Motion of Points, and on Universal Gravitation. Including the principal Propositions of Books I. and III. of the Principia. The first part of a Treatise on Dynamics. Third Edition. 8vo. Plates, 10s. 6d.

Whewell (Dr.) On the Motion of Points constrained and resisted, and on the Motion of a Rigid Body. The second part of a Treatise on Dynamics. Second Edition. 8vo. Plates, 12s. 6d.

Whewell (Dr.) Doctrine of Limits, with its Applications; namely, Conic Sections; the Three First Sections of Newton; and the Differential Calculus. 8vo. 9s.

Whewell D   Anal tical Statics.

Whewell (Dr.) Mechanical Euclid,
containing the Elements of Mechanics and Hydrostatics, demonstrated after the manner of Geometry. Fourth Edition. 12mo. 4s. 6d.; or with Supplement, 5s.

Whewell (Dr.) Remarks on Mathematical Reasoning
and on the Logic of Induction; a Supplement to the Fourth Edition of Dr. WHEWELL's Mechanical Euclid, containing the omitted parts of the Third Edition. 12mo. 1s.

Whewell (Dr.) The Mechanics of Engineering,
intended for use in the Universities, and in Colleges of Engineers. 8vo. 9s.

Willis (Prof.) Principles of Mechanism.
8vo. 15s.

Wood (Dean). Elements of Algebra.
Revised and enlarged, with Notes, additional Propositions, and Examples, by T. LUND, B.D., Fellow of St. John's College. 8vo. 12s. 6d.

Wood (Dean). Appendix to Algebra.
Containing Solutions of difficult Equations, and Problems, together with a large collection of Examples in every part of Algebra, and College Examination Papers, by T. LUND, B.D. 8vo. 6s. 6d.

Woodhouse (Prof.) Treatise on Plane and Spherical Trigonometry. Fifth Edition. 8vo. 12s.

Wrigley (A.) and Johnstone (W. H.) Collection of Examples in Pure and mixed Mathematics, with Hints and Answers. 8vo. 8s. 6d.

LIST OF MISCELLANEOUS WORKS,

RECENTLY PUBLISHED BY

J. & J. J. DEIGHTON,

Agents to the University,

CAMBRIDGE.

Alford (Rev. H.) The School of the Heart, and other Poems, 2 vols. 12mo. 8s.

Archæological Journal.
Published under the direction of the Central Committee of the Archæological Institute of Great Britain and Ireland for the Encouragement and Prosecution of Researches into the Arts and Monuments of the Early and Middle Ages. *Published Quarterly.* Nos. 1—7, 8vo. Plates, 2s. 6d. each, also vol. I. containing Nos. 1—4, with Index, &c., cloth, 11s.

Arnold (Dr Thomas). History of Rome.
8vo. vol. I. 16s. vol II. 18s. vol. III. 14s.

Arnold (Dr Thomas). History of the later Roman Commonwealth, from the end of the second Punic War, to the death of Julius Cæsar; and of the reign of Augustus; with a Life of Trajan. 2 vols. 8vo. cloth, 1l. 8s.

Biographical Dictionary.
A new General One, projected and partly arranged by the late Rev. HUGH JAMES ROSE, B.D., Principal of King's College, London. Edited by the Rev. HENRY J. ROSE, B.D. late Fellow of St John's College, Cambridge, 8vo. vols. I to VIII. 18s. each.
A volume is published Quarterly.

Butler (Bp.) Memoirs of his Life, Character, and Writings. By THOMAS BARTLETT, A.M., Rector of Kingstone, Kent. Portrait. 8vo. 12s.

Cambridge University Almanack for the Year 1846.
Embellished with a Line Engraving by Mr E. CHALLIS, from a Drawing by W. G. DODGSON, of the Great Court of Trinity College, 4s. 6d. Continued Annually.

Cambridge University Calendar, for the Year 1845.
6s. Continued Annually.

Cambridge Guide, including Historical and Architectural Notices of the Public Buildings, &c., *new Edition, illustrated by numerous beautiful Engravings, from Drawings by Mackenzie and Rudge, and a New Plan of the Town.* 12mo. cloth, 5s. 6d.

a   1 ge,   ustrations o .
Being a series of Views of the Public Buildings of the University and Town. Engraved by Messrs. STORER. 4to. and 8vo. *Each plate is sold separately.*

Cambridge Portfolio.
Consisting of Papers illustrative of the principal features in the Scholastic and Social System of the University. Edited by the Rev. J. J. SMITH, M.A., Fellow of Gonville and Caius College. 2 vols. 4to. with numerous engravings, &c. 4*l*. 4*s*.

Cambridge Antiquarian Society's Publications.

No. I.—Corrie (Rev. Prof.) A Catalogue of the Original Library of St Catharine's Hall, MCCCC.LXXV. 4to. sewed, 1*s*. 6*d*.

No. II.—Smith (Rev. J. J.) Abbreviata Cronica ab anno 1377, usque ad annum 1469. 4to. sewed, 2*s*. 6*d*.

No. III.—Goodwin (Rev. James). An Account of the Rites and Ceremonies which took place at the Consecration of Archbishop Parker, with an Introductory Preface and Notes. 4to. sewed, 3*s*. 6*d*.

Nos. IV. and V.—Woodham (H. A., Esq.) An Application of Heraldry to the Illustration of various University and Collegiate Antiquities. Part the First, 4to. sewed, 6*s*. Part the Second, 4to. sewed, 4*s*. 6*d*.

Nos. VI. and VIII.—Cowie (Rev. Morgan.) A Descriptive Catalogue of the Manuscripts and Scarce Books in the Library of St John's College, Cambridge. Parts I. and II. 4to. sewed, 4*s*. 6*d*. each.

No. VII.—Willis (Prof.) A Description of the Sextry Barn at Ely, lately demolished. With Illustrations. 4to. sewed, 3*s*.

No. IX.—Willis (Prof.) Architectural Nomenclature of the Middle Ages. 4to. Plates, sewed, 7*s*.

No. X.—Dryden (Sir Henry, Bart.) Roman and Roman-British Remains, at and near Shefford, Co. Beds.
King (C. W. Esq.) A Catalogue of Coins from the same place. 4to. Plates, sewed, 6*s*. 6*d*.

No. XI.—Smith (Rev. J. J.) Specimens of College Plate, with Thirteen Plates. 4to. sewed, 15*s*.

First Report, presented to the Cambridge Antiquarian Society, at its General Meeting, May 6, 1841. 8vo. sewed, 1*s*.

Second Report, presented May 13, 1842. 8vo. sewed, 1*s*.

Third Report, presented May 24, 1843. Sewed, 1*s*.

Fourth Report, presented May 14, 1844. Sewed, 1*s*.

Fifth Report, presented May 9, 1845. Sewed, 1*s*.

Corrie (Prof.) Brief Historical Notices of the Interference of the Crown with the Affairs of the English Universities. 8vo. 3s. 6d.

Dyer (G.) History of the University and Colleges of Cambridge; including Notices relating to the Founders and Eminent Men. 2 vols. 8vo. Plates, 18s. Large Paper, 1l. 11s. 6d.

Encyclopædia Metropolitana, with Index.
Complete in LIX. Parts.
Or in Volumes:
Pure Sciences, 2 vols. Mixed and Applied Sciences, 6 vols. History and Biography, 5 vols. Miscellaneous and Lexicographical, 12 vols. General Index, 1 vol.

Fuller (Dr. Thos.) History of the University of Cambridge, from the Conquest to the year 1634. Edited by Rev. M. PRICKETT, M.A., F.S.A., of Trinity College, and THOS. WRIGHT, Esq., M.A., F.S.A., of Trinity College; with Illustrative Notes. With two Plans of Cambridge. 8vo. 12s.

Gibbon. The History of the Decline and Fall of the Roman Empire. A new edition in one volume, with some account of the Life and Writings of the Author, by ALEXANDER CHALMERS, Esq. F.A.S. 8vo. Portrait, 18s.

Jenyns (Rev. L.) Manual of British Vertebrate Animals: or Descriptions of all the Animals belonging to the Classes Mammalia, Aves, Reptilia, Amphibia, and Pisces, observed in the British Islands. 8vo. 13s.

Neale, (J. M.) The loosing of the Euphratean Angels. A Poem which gained the Seatonian Prize, 1845. 8vo.

Robertson (Dr. W.) Works. To which is prefixed an account of his Life and Writings, by DUGALD STEWART. A new edition, in one vol. 8vo. Portrait, cloth, 18s.

Smith (Rev. Charles Lesingham). Poetical Works. 8vo. 5s.

Smyth (Prof.) Lectures on Modern History, from the Irruption of the Northern Nations to the Close of the American War. Fourth Edition. 2 vols. 8vo. 1l. 1s.

Smyth (Prof.) Lectures on History. Second and concluding Series. On the French Revolution. Second Edition. 3 vols. 8vo. 1l. 11s. 6d.

Thorp (Ven. Arch.) A Statement of Particulars connected with the Restoration of the Round Church, by the Chairman of the Restoration Committee. 8vo. sewed, 2s. 6d.

Walmisley (Prof.) A Collection of Anthems used in

Walmisley (Prof.) Collection of Chants in use at the Chapels of King's, Trinity, and St John's Colleges. The Voice parts in Score, with an Accompaniment for the Organ or Piano-forte. To which are added the Responses used at Trinity Chapel. Imp. 8vo. 12s. 6d.

Whewell (Dr.) Architectural Notes on German Churches; with Notes written during an Architectural Tour in Picardy and Normandy. Third Edition. To which is added, Translation of Notes on Churches of the Rhine, by M. F. De Lassaulx, Architectural Inspector to the King of Prussia. 8vo. Plates, 12s.

Whewell (Dr.) History of the Inductive Sciences, from the Earliest to the Present Time. 3 vols. 8vo. 2l. 2s.

Whewell (Dr.) The Philosophy of the Inductive Sciences, founded upon their History. 2 vols. 8vo. 1l. 10s.

Whewell (Dr.) On the Principles of English University Education. Including Additional Thoughts on the Study of Mathematics. Second Edition. 8vo. 5s.

Willis (Prof.) Remarks on the Architecture of the Middle Ages, especially in Italy. 8vo. Plates, 10s. 6d. Large Paper, 1l. 1s.

Willis (Prof.) The Architectural History of Canterbury Cathedral. 8vo. cloth, 10s. 6d.

VIEWS

OF THE

COLLEGES AND OTHER PUBLIC BUILDING

In the University of Cambridge,

Taken expressly for the UNIVERSITY ALMANACK,

(Measuring about 17 inches by 11 inches.)

No.	Year.	Subject.
1—	1801	TRINITY COLLEGE—West Front of Library.
2—	1802	KING'S COLLEGE and CHAPEL—West Front, and Clare Ha
3—	1803	St. JOHN'S COLLEGE—Bridge and West Front.
4—	1804	QUEENS' COLLEGE—taken from the Mill.
5—	1805	JESUS COLLEGE—taken from the Road.
6—	1806	EMMANUEL COLLEGE—West Front.
7—	1807	PEMBROKE COLLEGE—West Front.
8—	1808	TRINITY HALL—taken from Clare Hall Garden.
9—	1809	SIDNEY SUSSEX COLLEGE—taken from Bowling Green.
10—	1810	CHRIST'S COLLEGE—taken from the Garden.
11—	1811	CAIUS COLLEGE—Second Court.
12—	1812	DOWNING COLLEGE—Master's Lodge.
13—	1813	St. PETER'S COLLEGE—taken from the Street.
14—	1814	CATHARINE HALL—Interior of Court.
15—	1815	CORPUS CHRISTI COLLEGE—Interior of Old Court.
16—	1816	MAGDALENE COLLEGE—Front of Pepysian Library.
17—	1817	SENATE-HOUSE and UNIVERSITY LIBRARY.
18—	1818	TRINITY COLLEGE—Great Court.
19—	1819	St. JOHN'S COLLEGE—Second Court.
20—	1820	MAGDALENE COLLEGE—First Court.
21—	1821	EMMANUEL COLLEGE—First Court.
22—	1822	KING'S COLLEGE—Old Building.
23—	1823	JESUS COLLEGE—taken from the Close.
24—	1824	QUEENS' COLLEGE—taken from the Grove.
25—	1825	OBSERVATORY.
26—	1826	CORPUS CHRISTI COLLEGE—West Front, New Building.
27—	1827	TRINITY COLLEGE—Interior of King's Court.
28—	1828	St. PETER'S COLLEGE—Gisborne's Court.

No.	Year.	Subject.
29	1829	KING'S COLLEGE NEW BUILDINGS and CHAPEL—ta from the Street.
30	1830	ST. JOHN'S COLLEGE—New Building.
31	1831	TRINITY COLLEGE—West Front of King's Court and Library
32	1832	CHRIST'S COLLEGE—New Buildings.
33	1833	KING'S COLLEGE CHAPEL—Between the Roofs.
34	1834	PITT PRESS.
35	1835	SIDNEY SUSSEX COLLEGE—taken from an Elevation.
36	1836	KING'S COLLEGE—CHAPEL, &c. West Front.
37	1837	ST. JOHN'S COLLEGE—New Bridge, &c.
38	1838	FITZWILLIAM MUSEUM.
39	1839	The NEW UNIVERSITY LIBRARY.
40	1840	CAMBRIDGE—from the top of St. John's College New Buildin
41	1841	CLARE HALL—from the Bridge.
42	1842	FITZWILLIAM MUSEUM. Entrance Hall and Statue Gallery
43	1843	TRINITY COLLEGE. Interior of the Hall.
44	1844	ST. SEPULCHRE'S CHURCH) as restored by the CAMBRID CAMDEN SOCIETY.
45	1845	CAIUS COLLEGE Gate of Honour. SENATE HOUSE and N UNIVERSITY LIBRARY.
46	1846	GREAT COURT OF TRINITY COLLEGE.

Nos. 1 to 25, inclusive ......, Price, Plain Impressions ...... 2s. 6d.
Proofs .... 5s. 0d.
Nos. 26 to 45, ——— ...... —— Plain Impressions ...... 5s. 0d.
Proofs .... 8s. 0d.
—— on India Paper...12s. 0d.